KOREA UP CLOSE

Photographic Encounters by Foreign Observers

Korea Up Close

Photographic Encounters by Foreign Observers

Compiled by Craig White

Published by **Seoul Selection**
B1 Korean Publishers Association Bldg., 105-2 Sagan-dong,
Jongno-gu, Seoul 110-190, Korea
Tel: 82-2-734-9567
Fax:82-2-734-9562
publisher@seoulselection.com
www.seoulselection.com

ISBN:978-89-91913-18-9 03980

Printed in Korea

KOREA UP CLOSE

Photographic Encounters by Foreign Observers

Compiled by Craig White

Seoul Selection

Photo Credits

David Smeaton. All Rights Reserved. http://www.super-dave.com

Ralph Pruszynski. All Rights Reserved.
http://www.pbase.com/koreanczyk

Mary Crowe. All Rights Reserved. http://www.maryeats.com

Derek Winchester. All Rights Reserved.

Ben Voborsky. All Rights Reserved. http://www.benvoborsky.com

Andrew White. All Rights Reserved.

Nayan Sthankiya. All Rights Reserved. http://www.nayansthankiya.com

Gregory C. Brundage. All Rights Reserved.

Kim Dammers. All Rights Reserved.

Craig White. All Rights Reserved. http://www.galbijim.com

Tonya Schwochert. All Rights Reserved.

Chad Walker. All Rights Reserved.

Peter Garnhum. All Rights Reserved.

KOREA UP CLOSE

Photographic Encounters by Foreign Observers

Contents

Contents

Preface

For the longest time, Korea was referred to as 'The Hermit Kingdom,' a moniker that still gets tossed around, but more often when referring to the North. Yet, due to the perpetual media shadow that North Korea casts over its southerly brother, there may be a habit to forget and be a little caught off-guard that the South is so deep in culture and tradition, that one can feel the 'Kingdom' on a daily basis. As a foreigner working, living, and traveling throughout this country, it is impossible to step outside of your home without realizing how thick the culture runs.

Whether you like it or not, it intoxicates you, fills your lungs when you breathe, rings in your ears when you walk past, smothers you like a wave, and encases you like a warm blanket. Many foreigners refer to this as the 'Korean Bubble.' You don't notice it as much once you've been in the country for a while, but as soon as you step out of it, you inescapably feel its absence.

The only thing for certain is that Korea burns an impression into all of us, and everyone has their own unique encounter with her. This book is a collection of stories and imagery from foreigners talking about their interactions with Korea, the impressions and memories that will never be forgotten.

Craig White

For those unfamiliar to the idiosyncrasies of the country, you are bound to get a little lost without the periodic references to the culture or language. In this regard, you may find yourself wanting to refer to a glossary. Our glossary is online, at *www.galbijim.com*, the portal for foreigners who live, work, and travel in Korea.

A Surge for the Senses

Faces of Korea

Seoul Streets: Part I

Seoul Streets: Part II

Mary Eats

What Do You Put in Your Mouth?

A Glimpse at Traditional Ceremonies

Faces of Korea

David Smeaton

I was lured to Korea in the autumn of 2001 by the promise of an upcoming World Cup. Like most foreigners, I knew very little about Korea until I arrived. Actually, I knew only three things about Korea then: 1988 Olympics, Kimchi and World Cup.

I have been in Korea for five years and have settled into a comfortable life here. Like any country, at first, the cultural differences took some time getting used to, but I have learned to love those differences about Korea even though they can be frustrating at times.

My love for Korea has grown and what I love most is its people. I have traveled to many countries, especially around Asia, but it is still the people of Korea that I feel most drawn to.

The following are the faces of Korea, those I am most passionate about in this amazing country, isolated on the end of a peninsula:

Face of Calm

The golden Buddha statue nearby my house is a sign of peace and tranquility. Buddhist temples and statues are a common scene throughout Korea, especially Seoul. Some of my favorite places in Korea are these temples. I particularly love visiting the Bongeun Temple in Samseong-dong and Jogye Temple in Insadong. Korea has a long tradition of Buddhism, Confucianism as well as Shamanism. During the past few decades, Christianity has also become a popular and booming religion.

Face of Summer

As everyone knows, Korea is hot during the summer. Everyone is looking for respite against the waves of heat that melt us down. This boy was standing inside a fountain. The water streaming over him kept him cool and happy. In the summer, it is common for Koreans to flock to the beaches, pools and public parks (with lots of shady trees) to escape the heat. Beaches in the country often claim crowds of half a million or more.

Face of Passion

The World Cup in 2006 was an event of high expectations for Koreans. Thousands flooded to City Hall and Gwanghwamun to see the games and celebrate with their fellow countrymen. This man showed his patriotism by wearing the Korean flag as he walked through the subway at City Hall Subway Station. On this evening, the "Red Devils" (Korean soccer fans) were victorious as Korea beat Togo, 2 to 1.

Face of Soul

One of my favorite people in Korea is the man, whose name I don't even know, playing his accordian in Jongno. He is there everyday without fail, happily singing and posing for the camera.

Face of Beauty

I love the contrasts in Korea, and there is nothing more fun than going to COEX and seeing a motor show and even take in the chrome and the gloss of beautiful models. In Korea, motor shows are photographer's dream arena. The COEX regularly holds events where among them, the motor shows are often the most popular.

Face of Brotherhood

I saw these two young men at an event in Seoul. They were serving in the military, yet enjoying a day out during a national holiday. Note how the balloons on their hats are in striking contrast to their uniforms. Two years of military service is a duty for all Korean men in their early 20's.

Face of Tradition

Korea has seen a growing number of diverse events throughout the country for the past few years. Many of them are reenactments usually performed for foreigners to raise awareness of Korea's long and rich history. This man was making rice cakes, with his wooden hammer pounding the steaming rice into a pulp. Yet, I was more amused by his face than his creation, a face of age and wisdom.

Face of Dedication

At Olympic Park, Jamsil. A man and his son are training on the circuits around the Peace Gate. In perfect synchronization, they skated at a lightning speed, the father urging his son to go faster. It is common for Korean athletes to spend as much time on their appearance as they do in training, which explains the carefully matched skatewear.

Face of Elegance

At a Buddha's Birthday celebration, a woman danced on stage in a flowing white gown worn over her hanbok. Her graceful moves and slow dances were beautiful as she dazzled the crowd. Many trained women performed at Buddha's Birthday events, of which the traditional dances, captivating music and beautiful clothing were enrapturing.

Face of Winter

Near my school, this girl had found a small hill of ice. Slippery as it was, she spent an hour sliding up and down it. She wasn't bothered by a stranger trying to take her picture. In fact, she enjoyed sliding straight towards me and nearly knocked me over. My favorite time of the year in Korea is when snow falls and turns her into a white wonderland.

Face of Nature

I love the Seoul Grand Zoo. My favorite animals there are the giraffes with their long graceful necks. The tiger enclosure is also great to watch: I caught this tiger glaring right at me.

Face of Change

When I first came to Korea, the Cheonggyecheon Stream area was a bustling road full of honking cars and street vendors. Now it is a beautiful tribute to the changes in Seoul. I love walking down by the river and I always stop at the crossing-stones to take pictures of people as they cross the river. The 'river walk', as it is commonly known, is over four kilometers long and snakes through the center of Seoul. It is a great place to walk, and it is often a center of events and attractions during Korea's national holidays.

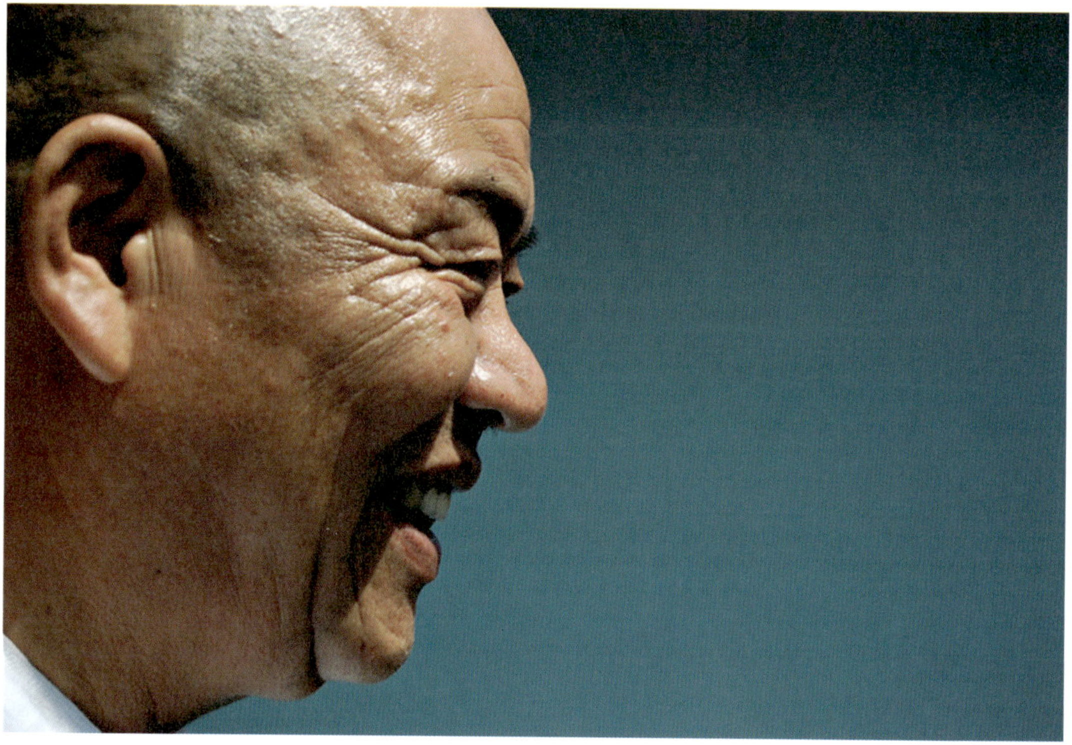

Face of Buddhism

This smiling monk is a friend of mine. He is from a small temple that houses a big golden Buddha near my apartment. The monk is always happy to see me and even though we cannot communicate freely, he smiles and shakes my hand to greet. Although the temple is quite small, the monk is warm-hearted and friendly.

Face of Art

Korea's art is truly spectacular with its rich and diverse artistic history. There are numerous artists who display their works to the public. This artist was drawing the Buddha. I was amazed by his graceful and skilled brush strokes.

Face of the Future

During the Buddhist celebrations, many monks from different countries visited Korea. This monk was really enjoying himself as he was shooting a video of his experiences. It was an unusual sight, to watch a monk hold a video camera and even wear a digital watch. It amazed me as I realized how quickly our world changes and how even old traditions embrace new, useful technologies.

Face of Formality

At City Hall, palace guards reenact the traditional guard exchange ceremony, while tourists look on. This man in full costume standing attentively at the gates of the palace is the head guard. It is always quite a spectacle to watch them march down towards Namdaemun.

Face Of Everland

Everland is one of Korea's most famous places and most foreigners venture out to this massive theme park. My favorite part of Everland is watching the polar bears. They enjoy catching small treats thrown by visitors. Here, the bear is waiting intensely for a snack to be thrown his way.

Face of Foreigners

There are a lot of foreigners in Korea nowadays. Many of us, like me, are teachers but some work in journalism, IT, global corporations, farms, or as entertainers. This man was hired by Everland as an entertainer. During a Halloween festival, he juggled balls and amused the crowd with his acrobatics and tricks.

Face of Music

At a musical performance in Seoul, this girl performed a solo on a traditional Korean drum. Although the drum was double-sided, she moved her drumsticks from side to side with incredible speed, almost as much a blur to the eye as it was a blur to the camera. Drumming performances are common throughout Seoul, and they are always fascinating to watch.

Face of Femininity

A *hanbok* (traditional Korean dress) is worn with full headwear by a woman dancing for the crowd during a celebration in Seoul.

Seoul Streets: Part I

Michael Hurt

For a lot of reasons, Seoul is actually a photographic heaven, even if we have labeled it a metaphorical "Hell" of a place to live. Like many of the cities that inspired some of the great photographers of both yesterday and today — Paris, New York, Chicago — Seoul is a "perfect storm" of all the right factors combining in just the right way to make for a special, volatile mix.

This city has one of the highest population densities in the world (take a look at Myeongdong on a weekend afternoon), and its landscape is so diverse, considered in terms of the dense, old streets of everyday neighborhoods, which stand in sharp contrast to the stark braggadocio with which the Tower Palace apartments seem to jut into the sky in the neighborhood of Dogok.

The difference between Seoul both north and south of the Han River is almost great enough to define two separate cities, both in appearance and atmosphere; the people who live and work in these two areas tend towards difference as well.

In Seoul, there are the well-coifed and meticulously kept housewives who keep the high-class Shinsaegae Department Store in business, as well as similar-aged women who hawk their various wares and trinkets on vinyl mats on the sidewalks outside of subway stations.

In addition to the rich and poor, you can see the generation gap between young and old, with old women stooped over from lack of calcium and hard labor, being passed on the streets by pretty young girls with long legs and backs made straight by the good nutrition and leisurely lifestyle enjoyed by any developed nation.

This is a country in which many people still spit on the sidewalks (something against which there were national campaigns to stop in the first years of the 1900's), yet one can also expect to find a wireless internet connection almost anywhere where there is a crowd.

The collision of old and new, traditional and modern — these themes have been talked about in regard to Seoul and Korea to such an extent that I don't really need to dwell upon it in depth here. But one thing that needs to be pointed out is that photographically, the contrasts and contradictions, the crowds and constant congestion, combined with the everyday clamor of rush hour, people bumping into other, the frustration caused by long lines, or waiting for a late friend — these are what makes Seoul a heaven to a photographer.

The urban landscape captures something essentially Korean in this mish-mash of everything from pre- to post-modern. The developed landscapes of Paris or New York, no matter how old and charming those two urban areas (as modern cities, they are far older than Seoul, actually, especially considering the physical destruction of the Korean War, as well as the fact that much of modern Seoul didn't exist before the 1970's), cannot compare to Seoul.

The essence of Korea's story, in terms of its compressed development and being the most quickly modernized and developed nation in the world, can be told by watching its people, knowing its streets.

Seoul Streets: Part II

Ralph Pruszynski

I have been a resident of Seoul for almost three years now. It is a city that I have a great affection for, because in a way it has retained much of its old charm, despite the destruction it has witnessed in its recent history.

Of course, on the other hand it is also a modern metropolis, always developing and changing. Nevertheless, even with all that change, some elements of the city remain the same.

I am especially interested in those areas of Seoul facing extinction. The remnants of the old city that are now being swept aside, as room is made for new developments. Although these developments are positive in the big picture, it comes at a cost, as the city sheds its older neighborhoods where we can still glimpse what life was like several decades ago.

I want to show that Seoul is beautiful and full of life, that it is not limited to Insadong, Gyeongbokgung Palace or the Blue House that are worthy of its own pride, but the city as a whole. Not all neighborhoods may look beautiful, but they all have their individual spirit and character, evolved over decades of post-Korean War existence. I hope that Koreans see this and that future development of the city is considered with this in mind.

I have been walking the streets of Seoul for the past year or so with a more or less clear goal. I wanted to use my camera to document this city that I have come to consider my home. Here are the results of my work so far; the old, the new, the everyday Seoul that I love.

Stroll by the Han River

A man enjoys a stroll by the flooding Han River. In the summer of 2006, Korea was hit by heavy rains which led to severe flood damage throughout some parts of the country. Although not the heaviest hit region, Seoul still suffered quite a damage.

Flood near Incheon Station

This is the aftermath of a heavy rainfall. A cigarette in hand, a man inspects the damage. The river spilled its banks and large parts of the riverside were flooded.

Onlooking the Horizon

A man enjoys fishing by the Han River.

A Runner's Path

A jogger races along the Han River. Seoul has a very well-developed riverside, with jogging paths, soccer fields and parks lining both sides of the Han River. It is popular for recreational activities among the inhabitants of Seoul.

The Sloping Horizon

Enjoying a cool day and a nice view, an angler waits patiently for a fish to be caught.

Seoul International Marathon

Korea holds international races that enjoy a lot of popularity both among the locals and foreigners.

Summer

A man enjoys a break on a bench while a cyclist speeds by. The summer of 2006 was characterized by heavy rains in the first half and then extremely humid and hot weather in the second half.

Spring Fever

A couple cuddles on a bench by the Han River in Yeoido while enjoying their date.

Dongdaemun Morning

A man prepares his street vendor on the street at a Saturday morning. The empty streets will soon be congested with traffic.

Seongsu-dong Alleyway

A father and son speed by on a motorcycle.

Trashman

A man pulls a cart of trash across the train tracks near Seoul Station in Yongsan-gu. Older people are often seen doing such hard physical labor.

Groundskeeping

Again, old people can be seen doing a lot of manual work. The women here were laying grass on a dirt field.

White Gloves

Those are the ubiquitous white gloves worn by most manual laborers.

Modern Seoul

Samseong-dong in Gangnam, is one of the wealthiest areas of Seoul. Unlike some parts of Seoul, this is a very modern area full of skyscrapers. A reflection of a poster watches a man board a bus by COEX, a huge complex of underground shopping and exhibition halls.

Gangnam

Gangnam is the most affluent areas of Seoul. Imported luxury items are a common scene in this area which consists of expensive shopping and real estate. Apartments here have recently seen their value skyrocket despite the government's policies to combat such boom.

Soccer Idol

A woman idolizes a football star as she looks up at a poster of David Beckham.

Dongdaemun Stairway

A man heads up the stairs at a market near Dongdaemun. Many areas of Seoul are known for its large markets. Most of all, the area around Dongdaemun is famous for its diversified shopping, where anything from upscale fashion items, auto parts and Chinese medicines can be purchased at a reasonable rate.

Dongdaemun Gate

A deliveryman rushes by on his motorbike. Dongdaemun Gate at a distance, is one of Korea's national treasures. It used to be the major eastern gate into the city. Today it is located nearby large markets encircled with roads.

Motorman

Motorcycles are a ubiquitous sight in Seoul. They are used primarily for delivery due to their speed and swiftness. They deliver all sorts of stuff from small parcels to huge boxes.

Traditional Street of Culture and Art—Insadong

A man takes a rest in Insadong, one of Seoul's most popular tourist destinations. It has dozens of art galleries, antique shops and restaurants. It is also located in the heart of an old downtown area, near Jongno 3(sam)-ga Subway Station.

Insadong Alleyway

A man walks down an alleyway in Insadong.

Metaportraits

Cheonggyecheon Lovers

A couple enjoys a day at Cheonggyecheon Stream. The Cheonggyecheon Stream is one of the recent additions to the city. Covered by large motorway in the 1970s, it has been restored and has quickly become one of the favorite places in Seoul to spend time.

Hopping on the Stepping-stones

An Open-air Photo Exhibition Outside City Hall

Jamsil Gym

A man enjoys a traditional dance. The older generation is quite active in exercise and leisure activities. Unlike some of the younger Koreans, the older people are still connected to the traditions of Korea.

Math Exhibition

A man puts on a mathematics exhibition outside the subway station in Oryu-dong in western Seoul.

Vanity

A woman checks herself in the mirror. Now, this is a country where appearance accounts for a great deal.

The Subway— Korea's Main Public Transportation

The Arrival

A student of Ewha Women's University awaits a subway train.

Steep Korean Landscape

Seoul is a city built on hills. Korea itself is extremely mountainous as 60-70% of the land is occupied by mountains. One of the most striking things about Seoul is how so much of it is nestled in valleys or built on hills. Here an old man struggles to descend down a very steep alleyway in a northern Seoul neighborhood.

Mary Eats

Mary Crowe

Kimbap

I remember it like it was yesterday. It was my first month in Korea and my husband had brought me lunch.

"Here," he said, dropping the ubiquitous black plastic shopping bag on my desk. "What is it," I asked, peeking into the bag, skeptically.

"Sushi," he replied, nonchalantly, already unwrapping his.

"Nice," I said, approvingly. As I looked over at him, though, something was amiss. I watched as he dexterously lifted a slice of *kimbap*, a white circle encasing a kaleidoscope of ingredients to his lips. I protested.

"I am not eating that," I said, defiantly pushing the bag over to his desk.

"That is not sushi."

I did not take to Korean food well. I had been cooking a long time before coming to Korea and considered myself quite worldly with cuisines. To the delight of my husband and friends, I often set out piquant Thai green curries, smoky Indian dals and savory South American empanadas. I considered myself a master of the 12 plus ingredient recipe, none too exotic, or expensive.

My knowledge of the Korean palate was limited, but I nonetheless found the earthy pungency of fermented pastes, excessive use of garlic, green onion and chili, and the cuts of meat, still bearing resemblance to their former whole, plebeian.

After years of drooling over well-styled glossy photos of exquisitely executed dishes in American culinary magazines like *Gourmet* and *Bon Appetite*, I was taken aback at grilling my dinner in a restaurant, or having a bubbling cauldron set before me, fish backbone or head awkwardly protruding over the edge.

During breaks from class, my foreign co-workers and I would

fried tofu with soy sause dish

commiserate. Each took turns nostalgically describing favorite foods or missed ingredients from home while the rest of us knowingly nodded our heads, arms empathetically pressed across our chests. Every weekend I would trudge into Seoul on a hot tip as to where I could score some fresh thyme or tortillas.

A year passed and we moved. We moved into an expat-free neighborhood, and I took employment at a small school, where lunch was provided for the staff. Not wanting to be rude, I would nibble at the rice and side dishes, a smile plastered across my face, counting the minutes until I could run home and fix up some "real" food. Then one hot summer day the cook set out a dish of fried tofu simmered in a sweet soy sauce mixture. With one bite, the forced smile slid off my face, replaced by a look of beguilement.

Most Korean culinary converts are seduced by the assertive flavors of *galbi* marinade or the tender texture of bulgogi, but in this humble serving of bean curd, the Korean palate clicked. The balance of the six holy ingredients, soy sauce, garlic, green onion, rice vinegar, sesame oil and chili pepper, opened up the door that I had previously shut, locked, bolted, and blocked with heavy furniture.

Suddenly I was ravenous. Like a child insistently begging her parents for the latest new Barbie, I pleaded with co-workers to translate recipes from Korean culinary magazines. I clipped weekly recipes from the Korean dailies and snatched up every book from *Kyobo* Bookshop I could find on Korean cuisine, restaurants, and cookbooks.

The ingredient list for my care packages began to shrink. "Don't you need more herbs de Provence, some dried porcini mushrooms?" my mother would ask, concerned. "No, we're ok," I would say. Setting my gaze on a newly purchased, glistening, oversized plastic red tub of *gochu* (chili) paste.

About this time I began to review restaurants for the now defunct bi-weekly English magazine, *Seoul Classified*. Having a forum for my new dialogue with food made me even more excited to get out there cooking and eating. I stopped buying American culinary magazines, and spent more time wandering the aisles of my local supermarket, picking up odd and unfamiliar foodstuffs to examine.

Without being consciously aware of it, I began to consume kimchi with my meals; a condiment I had been known to push to the far edge of the table with the tip of my silver chopsticks, so as not to contaminate myself. The day I wandered past a kimchi counter in E-mart and found myself salivating, I stopped in a cold sweat. I had gone native.

This isn't to say I eat seaweed soup for breakfast or have my refrigerator stuffed with various *banchan* (side dish). I haven't tried eating live octopus or baby pig backbone soup. There are many people out there who have embraced Korean food in ways I never will.

Eating Korean was more for me than just survival or a good meal. I was scared and unsure if Korea was the place for me. To keep me connected to my home, I needed to hold onto the stance that Korean cuisine was sub par, fearing if I let go, I'd lose my identity. Letting down my culinary armor was how I let Korea into my heart.

I still hate getting pushed in the subway, being nearly mowed down by a cab driver, cut in front of in line and all the other little annoyances that come with living in Korea. But my moments of tenderheartedness come when I make eye contact with someone slurping down a cool bowl of *naengmyeon* (cold noodles) on a suffocating summer afternoon. Or when I witness the dabbing of a hanky on a sweaty brow while consuming *ddeokbokki*, I say to myself, I know that sweat. I go especially soft when the *ajumma* who refills my *banchan* with a knowing smile, pats my arm while I gush over how delicious her cucumber kimchi is.

naengmyeon (cold noodles)

As the humble flavor combinations of Korea made their way first into my mouth and then into my heart; I learned to stop observing Korea as transient, and let myself become part of it.

Dubujorim (Fried Tofu in Soy Garlic Sauce)

Active time 30 minutes.

Start to finish 45 minutes.

Serves two as a main dish.

Ingredients:

1 package of firm tofu

1/2 cup cornstarch

1/4 cup soy sauce

1 healthy tablespoon of *gochu* (chili) paste, or 2 tablespoons of chili powder

1 healthy tablespoon of minced garlic

1 teaspoon of sugar (if using chili powder, increase sugar to two teaspoons)

1 tablespoon of sesame oil

1/2 –1 cup of water

1/2 green onion (leek) sliced thinly

1 tablespoon of sesame seeds

1 red chili pepper sliced thin.

1. Open the tofu, drain, and cut into 2cm to 4cm rectangles. Pat the tofu with a clean kitchen towel or paper towels to remove as much water as possible.
2. Place 1/2 cup of cornstarch on a plate. Dredge the tofu, coating evenly.
3. Heat 3 tablespoons of soybean oil in a large frying pan over medium high heat. Add the tofu and fry 1-2 minutes per side, until tofu is golden. Remove tofu and drain on a bed of paper towels.
4. In a medium saucepan, combine the soy sauce, chili powder, crushed garlic, sugar, and sesame oil. Stir until sugar is dissolved. Add water. Taste sauce and adjust seasoning as needed.
5. Add fried tofu to the pot and simmer in the sauce 1 minute, stirring to coat.
6. Remove tofu and place on serving dish. Spoon sauce over the top, and garnish with green onion, sesame seeds and sliced chilies. Can be served over rice or served as a side dish.

What Do You Put in Your Mouth?

Joe McPherson

Liz shrieked, "They're moving!" The glistening gray tentacles squirmed under the cucumber garnish as if in confusion about what had just happened to them.

nakji (octopus) **cuisine**

Liz and Jeremy came to Korea without much desire to go beyond their familiar concepts of food. We changed that.

I have to admit that ordering a batch of lively-squirming octopus tentacles was pushing them too far since this was their first time eating *hoe* (raw fish). We took them out to one of the many restaurants that had the fish swimming vigorously in small aquariums. It took merely 5-minutes for it to be carried out onto a plate from there. The meal was full of both familiar and exotic dishes.

Before coming to Korea, I had little idea about what Korean food was. Yet I did have a passion for the new, unusual, and the sublime, when it comes to food. Sensation seekers have a lust for new and intense experiences. Some skydive, some bungee jump. Some people get into hardcore drugs. When I saw a video of Anthony Bourdain eating a cobra's beating heart, it was an epiphany. "I wanna do that."

Bourdain spoke truthfully when he said, "I'm always awake in Asia."

Living in Korea has been like immersing myself in a tub of icy water. I feel alive with the constant challenges. A perfect example of this was a typical lunch my girlfriend and I had. Her *kimchi jjigae* (kimchi stew) arrived, boiling at the table. On the other hand, my *naengmyeon* (cold noodles) arrived chilled in heaps of shaved ice.

Diners eat their boiling soups and shove grilled-at-the-table meat into their mouths with no sign of agony. When eating Korean food, it is common to give what I call "the Korean food expression." It is a look on the face that is a mixture of searing pain and glorious ecstasy. The flavors have to be strong, sour, hot, or bitter. The food is not subtle. It is the rawest passion I have ever had at the dinner table.

There is a reason that Korean food hasn't caught on in the West as quickly as Chinese, Italian, and Japanese food. It is definitely not accommodating to the suburbanites who think eating a fajita at T.G.I. McChilibee's is exciting. Yet, if you have ever acquired a taste for something like oysters, cilantro, or goat cheese, you know that the most sublime food requires patience, and experimentation.

A lot of westerners coming to Korea have trouble with the food. Others become enthralled by it. Everyone has a preference for, at least, one type of food that is unique. Kathy likes *mussam* (radishes marinated in wasabi), and asks for it everywhere she eats. River is addicted to pepper paste, even though she's allergic to it. Colin can't get enough *naengmyeon*. I myself am a big fan of raw crabs marinated in pepper paste and a raw beef and pear dish that beats the pants off of any Parisian steak tartare.

Most foreigners can't enjoy Korean food immediately. It grows on them. By the end of my first month in Korea, I could tolerate kimchi. My second month, I craved it. These days I can mark the time of year by how the kimchi tastes in restaurants. Oh, and it's amazing on the grill.

dwenjang jjigae **(fermented saybean stew)**

The problem a lot of westerners have with kimchi is not that it is hot. It's that it is fermented and smells strong. Korea's landscape and history have shaped its food culture to depend on preserved and fermented food.

Fermentation is good. It's what makes great cheese, great beer, and great wine. It breaks down barriers in foods to release more nutrients when you eat them. My feeling is that if you like a good strong cheese, you shouldn't have a problem with fermented cabbage and soybeans. A good stinky *dwenjang jjigae* (fermented soybean stew), like a beer cheese soup, it can be a bowl of heaven.

For people who treat eating like it's an extreme sport, Korean food levels with the X-Games. There is much here to challenge your conventional concepts of

***bbeondaegi* (pupa)**

food. This is a land where kids may turn down a slice of chocolate cake but ravenously rip apart a package of dried-buttered-cuttlefish. There are hot dog and donut vendors on the streets next to silkworm larvae (reminded me of overcooked shrimp). Restaurants draw in diners by displaying pictures of what the food looks like before it is cooked. People dip raw hot peppers in hot pepper paste like ketchup on french fries.

Korea has the manliest of man food. Cow intestines are grilled in *soju* served with side dishes that include sliced-raw-liver. The shellfish spits hot juice dangerously at the diners in revenge of being roasted on glowing charcoals. Then there is the *ppyeodagui-haejangguk* (hangover stew) with caveman-esque hunks of pork spine and a broth made with clotted ox blood. This stuff would make a five-year-old hit puberty.

Let's not forget the ultimate taboo dish that Korea is infamous for – dog meat. It is a specialized dog breed that is bred only for meat, not as pets. It is the same difference between eating tuna but not eating goldfish. And, yes, I try to avoid places that has been known to serve dog that has been slaughtered in inhumane ways. I am politically progressive, but I think it is just ignorance and cultural arrogance that drives communities and activists to ban dog meat in the West.

The idea of eating dogs has been swept under the rug in recent years because of the negative attention it drew. I've run into more foreigners than Koreans who have eaten it and liked it. If raised and slaughtered humanely and cooked right, it tastes like a delicate pork. I have adopted a suggestion that we call dog meat "dork," as in calling pig meat, pork. If you're having such a problem facing the fact that you're eating an animal, dog meat can be renamed to make it less threatening.

My time in Korea has changed my eating habits and I don't think I can ever go back. Even though the flavor of Korean food is strong, it is also healthy. Korea is known for its barbecued meat. Yet even at galbi restaurants we wrap the meat in lettuce leaves, rice, and kimchi-like little fajitas. I eat a lot less meat than I used to though I am far from getting my Carnivore's Card revoked. My meat intake is more balanced than it was before. I've actually lost weight. I don't have the acid reflux problems I had on an American diet. And there ain't no way I'm gonna give up my kimchi, dammit!

Korean food and culture challenges you in ways that you're unprepared for. You realize that the world you knew before was just a backyard. You see how small you are in this world and come to terms with your insignificance. This realization is strangely liberating. You throw off the cultural chains that limited you and then you truly experience life.

Jeremy and Liz started this path toward the awakening that night. They didn't know that the Korean-style sashimi (*hoe*) meal was going to lead them to enjoying some grilled shellfish a month later. There was a moment when I saw the debate in their eyes. "Shoud we persist that the squirming octopus tentacles were disgusting, or figure out why people like them so much?'

Jeremy put down his chopsticks, picked up a tentacle, dipped it in sauce, and downed it. "How is it?"

"Chewy. Good."

A Glimpse at Traditional Ceremonies

Derek Winchester

I have been here for eight years and I didn't really see anything traditionally Korean until I put a camera in front of my face. I have read that a camera acts as a buffer to what you are seeing. For me it has been a frame. I feel like I can appreciate the country more when I am trying to capture the best photo possible. I am very lucky to be living in Suwon right now because there is a performance every Saturday, not very far from my apartment.

Suwon Dragon Decoration

Taken at the festival in Suwon.

Historical Examination

This shot is of a re-enactment of a historical civil service test.

Traditional Drummer

This is a crop of a drummer during a drum show. I really like how the eye in the dragon and the eye of the drummer line up.

Taken during the same drum show. They really went at those drums. I have never seen performers playing an instrument with such excitement.

'Skinship'

These two were getting ready to take part in the lantern festival parade. I really like the closeness in this shot. Between friends, there is something called 'skinship' but what it really is, is just being affectionate to one another.

Traditional Beauty

I was trying to get the lines of the hat and the lines of the lantern overhead to draw attention to her face. This was taken prior to the lantern parade.

Mini-monks

Latern Parade

Kids holding Jogyesa Temple laterns at the parade.

The Full Line of the Drummers

This is a great combination of dance and drumming. The drummers show off their elegant yet firm skills to the audience.

Civil Servant Exam Re-enactment Site

There were so many photographers there that I really had to make an effort without any of them actually in the shot.

This guy on the right would come around and make sure the writers had everything they needed.

Bongeunsa Temple

This is a shot of a woman in front of Bongeunsa Temple behind the COEX Mall. I really like the reflection in the red floor tiles.

An Old, Wiselooker in a Traditional Uniform

Tradition and Art Up Close

Far from the Maddening Crowd

Three Thousand Bows

Stillness of Dawn

Thwack of an Arrow Beats the Day

Cheon Han-bong, the Living Saga of Pottery

The Thousand Character Classic

Lords of Swords

Far from the Maddening Crowd

Aly Young

In Korea, there are an abundance of Buddhist temples to explore throughout the country. But as a foreigner wanting to experience Buddhist meditation and Dharma Talks in English without doing a temple stay, there are limited options.

However, during my first month in Korea, I was lucky enough to stumble into the Seoul International Zen Center located at Hwagyesa Temple in northeast Seoul.

Every Sunday from 1 pm to 3 pm, foreigners and Koreans alike can sit and meditate together in 30-minute periods, separated by 10 minutes of walking meditation. At 3 pm, a Dharma Talk is given in English, usually with consideration that there will be newcomers to Buddhism in the audience.

The temple was founded in 1523 by Master Shinwol, burned down in 1618, then was rebuilt the following year. It fell into disrepair and was reconstructed in the late 19th century. It now houses several famous statues, including a carving of the Bodhisattva Kstitigarbha, as well as two urns donated by the Queen Consort of King Honjong.

I found Hwagyesa Temple five months ago and have since been to many Sunday meditations, Dharma Talks and even a weekend of *Kyolche* with the monks. During that weekend, I woke at 3:30 am and participated in chanting, bowing and up to nine hours of meditation each day.

Kyolche translates into 'Tight Dharma' and refers to a 90-day summer and winter retreat when monks spend the majority of each day meditating.

It was a new experience to have such intense, disciplined introspection. Whenever I had previously thought about long hours of meditation, I had imagined a rather undeviating experience of sitting and merely clearing my mind. However, the roller coaster of thoughts and emotions that I actually experienced, were quite far from what I actually expected.

In the beginning, I went to the temple out of curiosity. I continue to go because of the all-encompassing question that Buddhism has sparked within me: What am I?

The chaos of the city melts away within the serene confines of Hwagyesa Temple, although it is just a short walk from the crowded streets of Seoul.

When I walk through the temple gate on Mt. Samgaksan, I feel detached from the rather contrary city life. A stream runs alongside the path to the temple, while the path leads to one of the entrances to Mt. Bukhansan National Park right before reaching the Main Buddha Hall.

The meditation begins with the hollow wooden beating of the *moktak*. I sit propped up on a pillow in the half-lotus position and begin letting the thoughts and emotions collected in a week of teaching kindergartners and a lifetime full of attachments...gradually drift away.

Pursuing meditation has admittedly not been an easy undertaking, but the more I do it, the easier it becomes.

The Dharma Talk that follows is usually an hour long and then there are questions from the audience.

On this particular weekend, the room was crowded in anticipation of hearing the inspiring and entertaining words of Hyongak Seunim, the guiding teacher for Hwagyesa Temple.

He was born into a large Catholic family in New Jersey, graduated from Yale and received his Master's in Theological Studies from Harvard. He decided to become a monk after meeting Zen Master Seung Sahn (the founder of the Seoul International Zen Center) at Harvard. Since then, he has written the bestseller "Man Haeng: From Harvard to Hwa Gye Sah Temple" and translated several of Sahn's English-language works into Korean.

The DharmaTalk was unscripted and interactive, and many times drew laughter from the audience. Questions of innocence and evil, cartoons and killing and the impermanence of everything were all discussed. At one point, Buddhism was even related to The Matrix.

Hyongak Seunim answered many questions with a simple, "shut your mouth," and at one point asked a confused questioner to come up to where he was sitting so he could hit him with his wooden stick. However, he was not being rude, but rather simply wanted them to clear their thinking of preconceptions.

Besides being a very entertaining and passionate speaker, Hyongak Seunim carries significant meanings behind his words—ones that cannot be taught just by listening to his speech.

Three Thousand Bows

Aly Young

Early Saturday evening, I somehow found myself walking under the umbrella through light rain and rumbling thunder on the road to Hwagyesa Temple. I was sitting on the steps out front, when Bo-haeng Seunim drove up and asked me what I was doing here. I said truthfully, "I don't know."

"Good answer," he replied, "Take your backpack to room 1-3. Be upstairs by six."

By chance, I happened upon the last Saturday of the month, the day when 3,000 bows are done from 9 pm to 3:30 am I didn't realize this until Bo-haeng Seunim mentioned it. But once I arrived, I assumed I would be doing meditation, chanting and bowing on the regular *Kyolche* schedule. Nothing is crazy like 3,000 bows without any mental preparation.

At 6 pm, I went upstairs for chanting and then again at 7 for one hour of sitting. The hour felt like two and at the end, I thought I was going to fall asleep. I had an hour to rest before bowing, but I couldn't sleep, so I lay down and wondered if I should just stay in my own room.

Of course, I didn't. What follows is my (perhaps overly dramatic) experience of 3,000 bows.

Around 100 people came to the temple for bowing that night. We were in the main Buddha Hall on the third floor of the temple. A monk at the front keeps count by hitting a stick before each bow. Kwan Seum Bosal (chanting of the Buddhist Goddess of Mercy) is continually being chanted. The six and a half hours is split into six sessions with short breaks in between and a 30-minute break at the halfway point.

At the eighth bow, I lost count. Everything hereafter is an estimate.

At the twentieth bow, I thought, 'this isn't so bad.'

On the 180th bow, I look at the clock for the first time and think the glowing red 9:17 pm must be a joke. I was expecting it to be closer to 9:40 pm.

300th bow—The robe and pants I was given to wear were hot and slightly itchy. I look around jealously at everyone in a t-shirt. Sweat is starting to bead up and roll down my neck and forehead. Some hot drops fall from me as I bow down and I watch them soak into the pink cushion. They also get into my eyes which became salty and burning, making my vision a blur. A drop is perched atop my nose, teasing me for several bows until it falls to its death. I wipe my forehead and after the next bow I left four fingerprints behind. Now I think, why didn't I bring my water bottle?

400th bows—I'm right next to a door and I want to kiss the woman who finally opens it to let in a breeze. The rain is still falling lightly and lightening flashes intermittently, bringing me back to the moment.

Lots of thinking during the first period. "What will I do on Sunday night? What am I doing on Wednesday, the Election Day? What do I need to do before my friend arrives on Wednesday from Kansas? What am I doing after I leave Korea? Do I need a visa for Malaysia? My Lonely Planet Malaysia will be here next week! I better start researching. I can't believe I only have three months left before I leave! That means only 13 more weekends to go! What should I do on my week vacation in August? A trip to Jeju-do maybe..." There were incessant interlinking thoughts, many that aren't fit for meditating at a temple.

700th bow—I notice a small blister on my left middle finger from pushing off the wood floor as I stand up.

800th bow—My legs have become as sturdy as *ramyeon* (Korean noodles). Which, by the way, sounds delicious since I didn't eat dinner tonight.

900th bow—The blister breaks open. I try to start bowing without using my hands for support, which is how I should have been doing it from the start.

1500th bow—I close my eyes for the first time and start chanting 'Kwan Seum Bosal'. My concentration slowed down considerably that I forget about my legs hurting.

Halfway through, we get a 30-minute break. Someone brings in rice cakes (the red bean kind that misleadingly look like brownies) and there is a huge container of some sort of sweet tea that everyone drinks out of bowls. I walk downstairs to my room and my legs are involuntarily shaking. At 12:30 am we start again.

Somewhere during the last three sessions, I started to have what I would call auditory hallucinations. In order to finish, I had to exert all my energy towards the bows with hardly anything left to think.

3000th Bow—The three clacks at almost 3:30 am signaled the end. I hobbled down the stairs and to my room to crash.

Stillness of Dawn

Ben Voborsky

Deoksugung Palace

It always amazes me when I find a quiet place in Seoul, in a city where there are people everywhere, I cannot pass up this chance to capture the stillness of life.

Children's Grand Park

It was a hot summer day and the sun very bright. Children played in the water and on the playground. This boy was catching some shade.

Tea Ceremony

The tea ceremony developed under the influence of Zen Buddhism. The aim is to help purify the soul by becoming one with nature. They are a delight to watch.

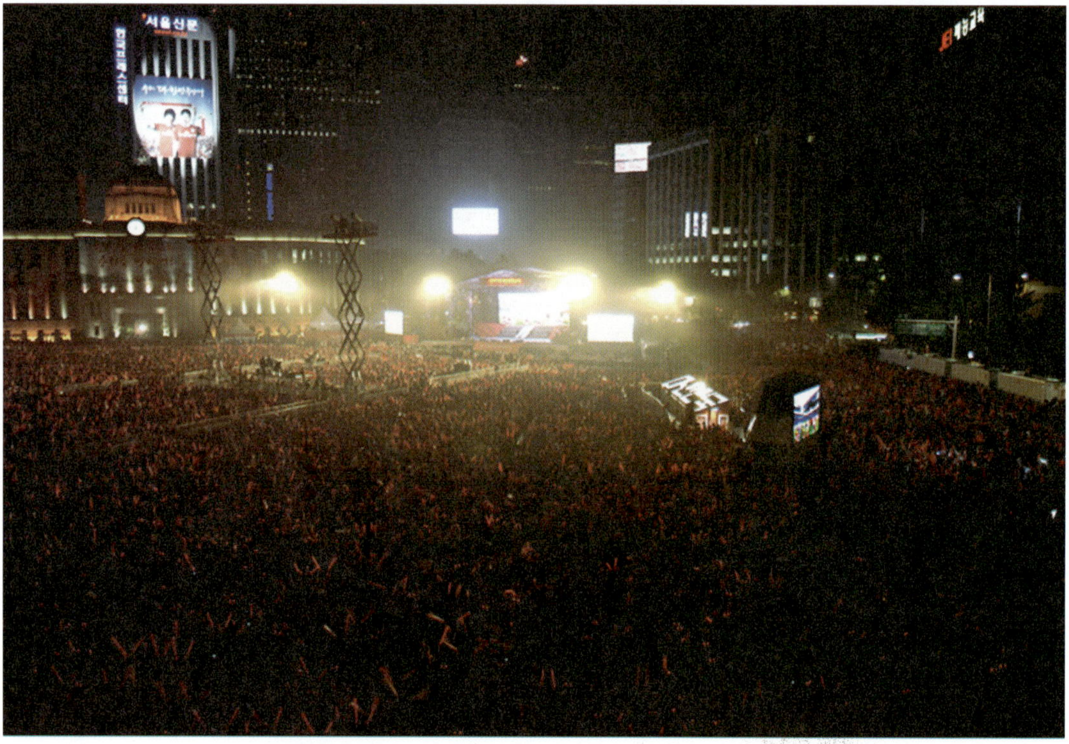

The Swarming Red Devils

Koreans are still football crazy. This is a view from the balcony of the Seoul Plaza Hotel, just across from City Hall. Taken at 4 am during the game between Korea and France at World Cup 2006.

Bouldering Competition at Seoul Plaza

The 2nd annual Seoul International Bouldering Competition was a huge success. International and Korean climbers participated in the two day event. The event was televised and the media was on hand. The routes were severely overhanging and extremely difficult. Some climbers tape their fingers before climbing to help support the tendons which suffer when hanging from your finger tips. Each climber has his or her pre-climbing ritual. Most include looking at the holds and visualizing the moves. But every climber chalks their hands. This keeps hands dry.

Buddhist Calligraphy-carvings by Ven. Hae-an

Prayer Beads by Ven. Hae-an

A Latern from the Latern Festival

Thwack of an Arrow Beats the Day

Andrew White

The Avid Author Aiming For an Accurate Shot

FFFFFSSSSSSSTTT...................TTTTHHHWWWAAAAAACCCKKK.......... I release the arrow and it flies off, first over the finely cut grass of our archery grounds, then over farmers' plots of cabbage, pumpkin, and radishes and over the meandering creek that winds through the valley.

The trajectory's apex reaches the height of the tree tops that form the "V" of the valley, the arrow flying straight. Then it slides down, over more gardens and the distant clearing, until it slams into the 2 by 3 meter wooden target, rebounds off and settles in the sand. The arrow flew 145 meters (159 yards- roughly a football field and a half) in a little over two seconds. Score one point.

This is Korean traditional archery, also know as *Guk-gung*. Unlike Western archery, with its focus on hunting, Korean traditional archery is a target-only sport, stemming from thousands of years of history as a military weapon. The bow, a recurve-laminate-style, comprised of wood, carbon, and layers of glass, has kept its traditional look. The outer-layer is covered with birch bark. Absent are the stabilizers, pulleys, and sights found in Olympic-style archery, which makes accuracy and technique all that more important.

I have been a member of Seoul's Surakjung (Surak Traditional Archery Club) for about four years, after being introduced to it by a Korean co-worker at the college where I teach. It is one of several clubs in Seoul, as every *Gu* (district) in Seoul supports one, including Sukhojung on Namsan Mountain and Hwanghakjung, located over a hill behind Kwanghwamun Gate. In total, there are over 200 traditional archery ranges in Korea.

For me, nothing beats being able to sneak away from work for a couple hours, get out of the crowd and hassle of the city, and shoot some arrows in the quiet mountains. I have seen deer come down from the woods and I threatened them back up again as I retrieve my arrows. I hear the 'clock, clock, clock' of the monk's *moktak* (wooden gong) from the surrounding temples, as the sunlight fades and the shadows cover the valley. The magpies dart and swoop, and hop around on the grass lawn in front of the shooting line. And I drink mountain water from a gourd.

Various Arrow Belongings

The beautiful scenery helps, but it is mostly about the archery. Nine sets of five shots, forty-five total possible hits are considered a full scorecard. I like the concentration—the constant focus on technique, the suspended animation as the arrow silhouetted in the sky, flies at a speed one notch less than a bullet, toward the distant target. I feel instant gratification upon hearing the THWACK of the arrow hitting the target 145 meters away.

Cheon Han-bong, the Living Saga of Pottery

Nayan Sthankiya

Having spent five years in Korea, I have covered various aspects of Korean life. On the international stage as well as the local, Korea is on a break-neck pace to become the darling of Asia and the hub of commerce and technology, often at the exclusion of its own unique cultural and artistic identity. To this end, I am submitting images of the cultural and artistic masters of old Korea, the techniques and traditions that are rapidly disappearing in modern Korea.

Cheon Han-bong has been making pottery most of his life and is renowned in Japan and Korea for his tea bowls, which command $500,000 each in Japan. They are so highly prized by the Japanese that many buyers come directly to his studio in Korea, choosing their pieces even before they have been unloaded from the kilns.

Cheon Han-bong takes a break after unloading the kilns.

Cheon Kyung-hee continues to load wood into the kilns while her father takes a short break.

The kiln, loaded with tea bowls, glows a molten red as the glaze reacts to the heat of the kilns.

Cheon Kyung-hee watches over the kilns and adds the last of the wood, taking over from her father who had already worked 12 hours this day.

Cheon Han-bong towels off after exiting one of the kilns.

Tea bowls
unloaded from the
kilns and waiting
the final inspection
and finishing.

Tea Bowls and Tea Sets

Cheon Han-bong picks his six best bowls from the hundreds that have been fired.

Cheon Han-bong examines each piece and sets aside those that do not meet his exacting standards. They will be destroyed.

Cheon Han-bong kneels over broken shards of his pottery. He destroys all pieces that do not meet his high standards of quality.

The Thousand Character Classic

Donald Anderson

"Being infinitely vast, the sky is black. There being nothing lower, the ground is yellow. In this space between infinite and the Earth, the universe overflows with a wild and unharnessed energy."

And so begins the Thousand Character Classic (千字文). Long before TOEIC and TOEFL came onto the Korean education scene, this classic has dominated Korean academic life. Until the 20th century, the vast majority of all documents written on this peninsula were one hundred percent composed by Chinese characters. The characters were conveyed to Korea via various classics of Chinese philosophy. One of the first and primary sources of Chinese characters in Korea was this classic. The first character of its title '千' means Thousand, the second '字,' Letter, and the third '文,' Text. True to its name, it is a text composed of exactly one thousand Chinese characters. Each character is unique, occurring only once within the text.

The Thousand Character Classic made its way to Korea in approximately the 6th Century. It was used as a primer for learning Chinese characters. From the 16th century to the early 20th century, it was required learning for Korean students. Students would memorize the characters by song or by chanting, saying first the Korean meaning of a character, followed by the character's pronunciation.

Its thousand characters can be subdivided into 250 sets of four characters each. The themes are a multitude. It contains statements of ethics and morals, basic observations about the world, specific notes about obscure ancient events in China, and other notes about language itself. In some cases, the meaning of some of the quadruplets can quickly be deduced if you know the meaning of the four characters: sea-salty-river-tasteless. 'Sea water is salty, while river water has no taste.' Other quadruplets need an explanation, especially when one of the characters refers to a forgotten historical figure's name, or the name of a no longer existing place.

At the beginning of the 21st century, more than 1,400 years after its conception, why is this classic still relevant? The question is not easily answered, except to say that by their nature, the Korean people do not seem to let a thing disappear easily once it has become entrenched. In regards to Chinese characters, Korea has zealously maintained their original strokes from ancient times, while China itself and Japan have simplified many of them. In terms of the Thousand Character Classic, Koreans seem to follow a law that says "once a classic, always a classic." In China, however, the Thousand Classic is seen as just another classic amongst many classics. It seems to be little studied by Western scholars, judging by how sparse references to it are in English literature. In Japan, the text seems to have some relevance for calligraphers, since the thousand characters have almost entirely become important, classic characters.

My own interest in the Thousand Character Classic began a few summers ago when two completely unrelated books I was reading both referenced it. One of these was the book Lost Japan by Alex Kerr, the well-known Japanologist. The other reference was in the Marok Biographies, one of the books in a series of Korean literature sold in pocketable format for 5,000 won. Take a trip to any Korean bookstore and ask about it, and you should find five to fifteen books concerning it. On subways in Seoul, vendors move up and down the cars trying to sell things to passengers; on several occasions, I have seen the vendors selling guides to the Thousand Classic. Despite the widespread availability of the classic, I do not encounter many Koreans who can read it beyond the famous first four characters: sky, land, black, yellow. Older Koreans claim to have studied it in their school days, but seem to have forgotten about it. The Thousand Character Classic can be likened to some ancient Greek text, which every intellectual means to read but has not.

Modern society advances at an increasingly alarming speed that we are forced to multitask to keep up. New technologies increase our output, but overwhelm us with the task of maintaining things already in progress, while new ventures are always launching. It gets harder to keep our mind and bodies in the same present moment. For me, studying the Thousand Character Classic provides a good antidote to modern life. It is after all, just thousand characters. It feeds me with the pleasant illusion that knowledge can be categorized and memorized. Studying it also makes my life in Asia more interesting. When I visit a temple, palace or train station and see a Chinese character here or there, I habitually recognize its place in the Thousand Character Classic.

I leave you with this timeless wisdom from the classic: 'The treasures amongst fruit are the plum and the crab apple.'

Lords of Swords

Gregory Brundage & Kim Dammers

Korean Traditional Swordsmiths: The Revival of a Lost Art

Japanese Samurai swords are probably the most famous in the world. But it wasn't always so.

Stone Age swords in Korea date back to about 1,000 B.C. The first use of iron in Korea appears to have been sometime between the 8th and 4th century B.C. Korea has natural iron deposits which are relatively high in carbon. Unlike Chinese iron, Korean iron artifacts usually have greater than 0.5% carbon content. This forms the basis for strong steel and great swords.

During the third, fourth and fifth centuries, technologies learned in China passed to Korea and then Japan. One example is the remarkable seven-branched iron sword, still in the Isonokami Shrine in Japan, apparently sent around 394 to Japan from Baekje as a symbol of vassalage, alliance or respect between the two lands. Some scholars believe the "hundred-times wrought iron" (as inscribed on the sword) technology led to the flowering of Japanese iron technology. It appears that the iron used to make the first Japanese weapons came from Korea until about the fifth century.

The oldest swords in Korea are straight and double-edged. Korean curved swords came along in the late Goryeo Dynasty.

During the Goryeo Dynasty, Korean sword-making was heavily influenced by Mongolian sword construction and design. Lasting from about 892 A.D. to 1259, this dynasty ended with Mongolian domination of the peninsula. Though the Mongols failed to colonize Japan, various technologies from Genghis Khan's (1162-1227) empire including swordsmithing reached Japan and dominated sword design in the Kamakura region. Kamakura was the political center of Japan for about a century after 1192.

Korean curved swords can be distinguished from Japanese, in that Japanese curved swords usually have a longitudinal channel or blood groove along the blunt edge of the sword, whereas Korean curved blades do not. Also, Korean curved swords tend to be smooth from the blunt edge to the sharp edge, with no straight lines running the length of the blade.

Until the Joseon Dynasty (1392-1905), Korean sword makers were among the best in the world. Korean swordsmithing began its decline during the Joseon Dynasty when King Lee Song-gye began to transition Korea from a Buddhist to a Confucian nation. Neo-Confucianism led to official disdain for the arts of war. Prior to the Joseon Dynasty swordsmiths in Korea lived within the palace. At the time, they were relegated to one of the lowest ranks of society.

Consequently, while the militaristic society of feudal Japan encouraged weapons-making, the scholastic society of Korea despised it. Thus, Korean sword-making technology was left to stagnate.

About one hundred years ago, the

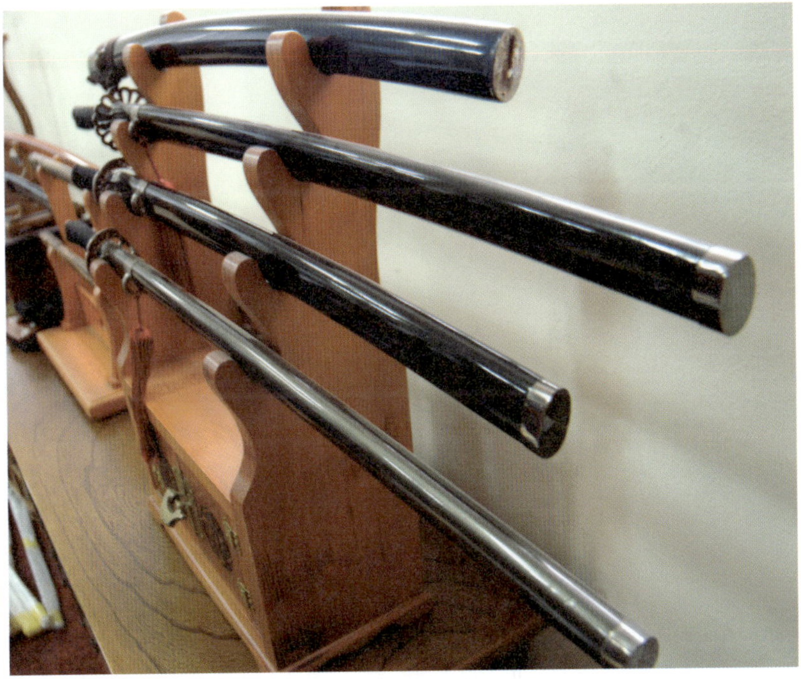

ancient methodologies of Korean swordmaking were lost altogether. Numerous factors were involved, including newer methods of steel production, the use of guns and the Japanese occupation of Korea. Korean swordsmiths were usually just killed.

During the last twenty years or so, the Korean sword industry has struggled to regain its former glory. This story is about our exhaustive search around Korea for its master swordsmiths.

Korea's Master Swordsmiths:

Lee Eun-cheul

About 20 years ago, a young artist named Lee Eun-cheul read an article about a man named Park Yong-ki who was making "Eunjangdo" knives. Though a ladies' weapon, historically this silver knife was lethal. Lee Eun-cheul was inspired by this article. But he wanted to go further; he

wanted to make swords using the ancient methods.

Thus began a quest by Lee Eun-cheul which was to occupy the next twenty years of his life.

Specifically, Master Lee set himself upon the task of rediscovering the ancient art and science of Korean swordsmithing in all its aspects. Even more specifically, he wanted to reconstruct the old ways of making Baekje and Goryeo Dynasty swords. According to Master Lee, sword technology in East Asia went from Korean Baekje Dynasty to Shilla Dynasty to Japan and then more recently, came back to Korea again.

Lee Eun-cheul usually mines his own iron. He digs it nearby his house. It is heavy, black and shiny. He said he needs about 6 kilograms of it to make two swords.

When finished, his swords are of high-carbon steel. It usually takes Lee Eun-cheul somewhere between three to six months to make one sword. The swords that he makes are not for sale. Some of his blades have been cut for scientific microscopic examination. This is useful to scientists who want to know about the metallic qualities of Korean traditional swords, because he uses the same methodologies in making his swords. Cutting ancient swords for examination would be criminal. Lee Eun-cheul, however, is aware of the needs of scientific curiosity and graciously allows some of his swords to be dissected for scientific purposes. This is the only place in the country where this old-style smelting is done. He uses the same smelting methods as the ancient (Baekje) process 1,500 years ago.

Though what appears to be bloom (ash and slag mix) can be found in his workshop, his blast furnaces are sufficiently hot enough that molten iron pours out. The melting point of pure iron is 1540°C. Repeatedly re-forging the iron in a carbon-rich environment makes a higher quality steel. Lee Eun-cheul then shapes the iron into four-sided rods. The rods are cut into short sections of about 8 cms and layered four or five deep in a criss-cross fashion. This is done to equalize the carbon distribution throughout the sword. This roughly cubical-shaped structure is heated together in a charcoal hearth with air forced in by wooden push-pull bellows and shaped into another rod which when heated cherry red is beaten into rough sword shape, dipped in ashes, heated, folded and beaten again and again. He usually does one or two quenchings in water. Usually there are three men helping him during the beating process. The strikers say "*Hanna, Dul, Set*" (one, two, three) in turn as they strike. It is almost like a dance. The master holds and turns the sword-to-be. (Modern swordsmiths usually use a "drop hammer"—a compressed air-driven forging hammer that drops vertically onto the work piece.)

When it is roughly shaped, he grinds and then polishes the sword. Lee generally uses Australian magnetite powder for the final silver finish. All of his swords are polished, but only a few have hilts and scabbards added.

After many years of research and experimentation with ancient iron and steel manufacturing techniques, Lee Eun-cheul went to Japan in 2002 to expand his study of traditional methods of sword-making. In Japan's Okayama Province, Lee Eun-cheul studied the sword-making practices of Sword Master Aoki Yutakasan, a famous Japanese swordsmith and member of the All-Japan Swordsmith Association.

The irony of this situation was not lost on Lee Eun-cheul, who realized that he had to go to Japan to rediscover Korea's forgotten swordsmithing skills, which were lost near the beginning of the Japanese colonization of Korea.

His work has been showcased in three documentaries, including the

MBC program "2580" in "2005: History Special Episode."

Lee Eun-cheul's title is *Dokeomjang* or traditional swordmaster. He is Korea's only traditional swordmaster at this time. To those who know him, and those who know of him, Lee Eun-cheul is known as a *muhyeong moonhwajae.* (intangible cultural asset)

Lee Sang-seon

Born in Chungnam Province in 1953, Lee Sang-seon became interested in swords when he was 18 years old. He said some of his family members scolded him when he was young for his interest in swords: "Sword-making is superficial and a waste of time," they said. But Lee Sang-seon continued when he realized that he had the skill to make steel, a good steel. Thus, undeterred by criticism, Lee Sang-seon went on to become one of Korea's finest swordsmiths.

Lee Sang-seon makes an amazing variety of swords and other weapons from various epochs in Korean history, mostly the Joseon era.

—Kings Sword (Saingeom)

Probably the most famous of his swords is the King's Sword called "Saingeum." "Sa" is a Korean word meaning "four" and refers to the four essential criteria used in its production. The King's sword can only be fashioned in 1) the year of the tiger, 2) the month of the tiger, 3) on the day of the tiger, and 4) at the hour of the tiger. Korean shamanistic beliefs contribute very much to the aura, mystery and power of this magnificent weapon. The last year of the tiger was 1998; the next will be 2010. A special ancestral rite must be performed when the sword is near being finished.

In Korean history, the king did not hand his sword down to his son.

Rather, it was buried with him, thus each king had to have a sword made especially for him. The length of the sword varied according to the taste of the king; however, the length was not supposed to exceed the distance between the sword held at the hilt while the arm is fully extended down, and the ear. Historically, a large-sized King's sword was about one meter in length. Lee Sang-seon's King's sword blades are 82.84 cm (about 33 1/2 inches) in length. The total length is 121.22 cm (almost 48 inches). The weight is a considerable 3.7 kg. (over 8 pounds)

—Subjects' Sword (Samimgeom)

These straight swords are based on the early Joseon era design. "Sam" means three and refers to the fact that they can only be made during 1) tiger month, 2) tiger day, and 3) tiger hour, unlike the Kings Sword which also has to be started in the Tiger year. Seventy cm (28 inches) in length, they are double-edged and weigh 2.2 kilos (almost five pounds).

—Kung Jung Yu Mul (Palace treasures)

These treasures included an amazing variety of weapons, from swords, to halberds, maces, axes, throwing stars and knives, spears, trident-like weapons and so on. Included in this group is a training sword (*suryongdo*) used in *geomdo* (Korean sword fighting) practice. It is this sword that is the bread and butter of Lee Sang-seon's craftings. Many *geomdo gwangjangnim* (masters) come to him for these swords. They are replicas of Joseon era swords that are made from more flexible steel necessary to endure the constant action to which they are subjected. They are of Joseon design and are curved similar to Japanese samurai swords.

—Admiral Lee Sun-shin's Sword

One of the more exotic swords that Lee Sang-seon has made includes replicas of Admiral Lee Sun-shin's ceremonial sword. It is approximately

1.97 m (6 1/2 ft) in length. He said it takes about six months to make one and sells for about US $8,000. The buyers have been wealthy sword collectors.

Lee Sang-seon gets his raw materials from the Pohang Iron Company, though, surprisingly, he gets his coal from Germany. It is a special coal that he says burns very hot and produces very little ash. He said he uses five materials in making a sword. He quenches it in motor oil.

Because he works alone, he can only work on a maximum of three swords at a time and it takes about fifteen days to complete a sword. Lee Sang-seon sells swords only upon request. He makes swords for specific customers and no two swords are exactly the same.

He received his license from the Korean government in 1989. He said that the background investigation required to get a license is exhaustive: they questioned him regarding his family history going back three generations, and also his wife and her family history. Then after passing this rigorous investigation, and paying a hefty license fee, the Provincial Chief of Police must approve the application. On a positive note, Lee Sang-seon said that the standards have relaxed a little over the years.

Asked about the differences between Japanese swords and Korean swords, Sword Master Lee said that Japanese swords were made for killing people, whereas Korean swords were made for saving people. He also mentioned that Japanese swords typically have a blood groove running along the top side of the blade. He added that Korean swords often had special lines, pictures or writings painted or etched on the blade, usually for shamanistic reasons.

He also mentioned that the Japanese government supports their manufacturers, whereas the Korean government has thus far not supported the indigenous sword industry.

In the year 2000, Lee Sang-seon moved from Incheon city to his current location, in Gyeongsangbuk-do Province, Mungyeong City, Uncheok-myeon Village. He lives and labors in an old school house complex which he has transformed into a workshop and museum of

Korean weaponry. As can be seen in the photos, Lee Sang-seon has created an awesome collection of very authentic looking replica weapons. Gyeonggi University in Gyeonggi Province (near Seoul) has bought a collection of about forty of his swords, which are on display there.

He is a kind and gracious host to those who visit him and his vast and breath-taking collection of ancient weapons.

Kang Cheul-kyu

Born in July 1956 in Yeosu City, South Jeolla Province, and the son of a Christian minister, swordmaster Kang Cheul-kyu is a modern master swordsmith. Like the swords he makes, swordmaster Kang Cheul-kyu is strong, direct and honest.

He started to learn about swordsmithing about twenty-five years ago. At the time, the economy in Korea was not so good and he was a young man in search of a mission and profession. Enters Mr. Yeon. Yeon In-moon is something of a legend in Korea. Several of today's Korean master swordsmiths learned their art from Mr. Yeon in Seoul many years ago. Now retired, he remains something of a mystery and is held in awe by his former students. Swordsmith Kang Cheul-kyu studied under Mr. Yeon for a little more than five years. At the end of this apprenticeship, he felt he had some creative ideas of his own he needed to develop and consequently moved on to further his own art. These ideas panned out into the creation of new and superior swordsmithing methodologies and designs and are now closely guarded secrets.

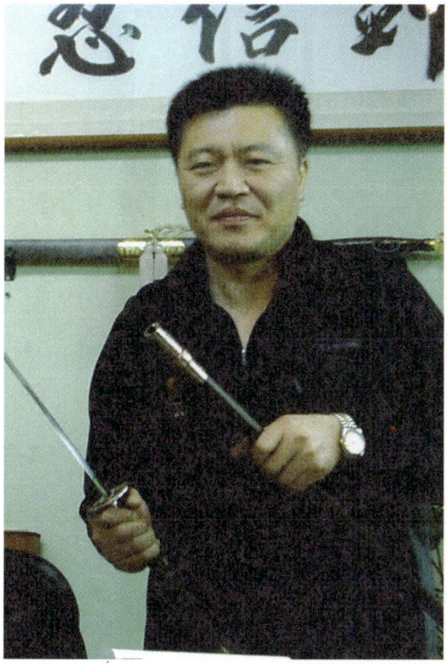

One difference, for example, between swordmaster Kang Cheul-kyu and most other swordsmiths is that he uses an electric furnace that he designed himself rather than the traditional charcoal or coal furnaces. He also uses three different baths for quenching, using different oils.

Asked about the materials he uses to make his swords, Master Kang reported that he uses three different kinds of steel: SK 3, SK 11 and something called tanjo steel. SK 3, SK 11 are stainless steels used for making normal quality swords. Tanjo steel, however, is very special. "Tanjo" means pounding. This is a special, very high quality steel that has been pounded vastly more than the ordinary quality steel. Tanjo steel swords, according to swordmaster Kang, are virtually immortal. He said that foreigners looking for swords always ask for "stainless steel," so they buy SK 3 or SK 11. Tanjo steel, however, is unique to Korea and Japan. Another unique quality of tanjo is that it "sweats" for several years. Consequently, this very special handcrafted weapon needs to be wiped down occasionally for a few years after its creation, to remove the light film that keeps accumulating. The SK 3 and SK 11 steels are bought from Japan. The steel that he uses to make tanjo weapons is from a Korean company, whose Master Kang prefers not to divulge.

Asked about getting a license to sell swords, Master Kang reported that the government had liberalized a little and police investigations into family histories were not as rigorous as in the past, though he said that the license still costs between US $20,000 to $30,000.

Queried about government support of Korean swordsmiths, he said that he believed the government doesn't like swords and only thinks of them as "dangerous." Asked if there were an association of swordsmiths in Korea, he said that there wasn't. "Korean swordsmiths are very individualistic," he added.

Swordmaster Kang Cheul-kyu has two technicians that assist him in his work. He currently produces about two hundred swords a year.

Ra Yeun-hee

Ra Yeun-hee is a rather unusual lady. At university she was trained to be a lawyer, a profession she excelled at. Then, six years ago in a rather unusual move, she went into the sword manufacturing business. Her husband, working at the Army College (*Yukgun Saguan Hakgyo*) in Daejeon City, encouraged and supported her all the way.

Today she works there with her brother-in-law, Kim Hyun-ik and a small staff producing beautiful Korean swords. Their shop is located in the small, scenic neighborhood of Shinseong-dong, in the suburb of Yusong, on the outskirts of the very large metropolitan city of Daejeon.

The surprises don't stop there. For example, she gets her iron from Germany and uses a German sword-making machine to produce swords with Korean designs. Her logic is undeniable. German steel and machine technology is certainly respected worldwide. Even Hyundai hires German engineers to work for them. The results can't be denied either. Her swords are strong, sharp and beautiful.

The company's mass-machine production of swords of ancient design allows them to make swords cheaper than the competition, and consequently, they do a high volume of sales.

If all this isn't amazing enough, Ra Yeun-hee and Kim Hyeok-ik were very modest about their business. They said they plan to move and upgrade all their systems within the next year or two.

For foreigners who would like to buy swords, this is a pretty good place, because Kim Hyuk-ik speaks English rather well, though again, he was very modest about it and kept denying it!

Like most people interested in swords, Kim Hyun-ik had a story to tell. He said it is true that Japanese historically have made great swords, but that Koreans in ancient times usually preferred bows and arrows to swords, partly because of Korea's mountainous terrain.

One of their more unusual swords is called *Tsam Po*. It actually has a triangular- shaped blade with three cutting edges. This is claimed to be modeled after an original Korean design. They also showed us a Hwando Dedo, or "big sword," modeled after a sixth century design. Then there is the "Chilsonggeum," or seven-star sword, originally made between 1561 and 1597. On the blade are etched, indeed, seven stars. What makes this sword really unique is that two swords fit into one scabbard. They are a perfectly matched pair. These four swords are collectors' items.

Asked about their most popular swords, they said two swords in particular have the highest sales volume.

First is the *Samkakdo*, a really sharp sword with a rather thin blade. It is mainly used by Hedong Kumdo people who practice poomses (pre-arranged sequences of attack and defense movements) with it. It is also good for the practice of slicing through bundles of tightly bound straw.

Second is the *Yukkakdo*, a sword with a thicker back, used by both Hedong and Taehan Kumdo people for practice for poomses and slicing through bamboo trees. It is not as sharp as the *Samkakdo* but holds its edge well through vigorous use.

Both of these swords look vaguely like Japanese samurai swords, but really are Korean designs. However, when requested by a customer, they do sometimes put a blood groove on the *Yukkakdo* sword because it makes a whistling sound during poomse practice.

These swords can be bought for between six hundred thousand won and eight hundred thousand won, about half the market price of similar swords.

One interesting difference they mentioned between Korean and Japanese swords is that in the Korean design they use two pins to attach the pommel to the steel sword handle, whereas they said Japanese swords usually use only one pin.

One of their more expensive swords looks a bit like the *Yukkakdo*, however is made with special tanjo steel and has gold inlay on the sword and sheath.

Han Jong-chil

Demonstrating the great significance of swords in Korean culture, upon promotion to a general or an admiral, the President of Korea awards to the officer a sword. This tradition dates far back in Korean history. Once upon a time, Korean kings awarded a sword to top commanders. This tradition was discontinued upon the demise of the monarchy in the early part of the twentieth century. It was revived in 1983 during the regime of President Cheon Du-hwan.

Since 1983, these swords have been slightly curved, similar to a Japanese sword. As of January 1, 2007, newly promoted Korean generals and admirals will be awarded a straight double-edged sword—a more traditional Korean design. When a general is promoted to three stars, he gets a red ribbon attached to the sword. On one side of the ribbon is written "the President of the Republic of Korea," on the other side is written the officer's position in the army. The same things apply for navy admirals. The swords apparently cost about 2 million won.

In 1995, the company that made swords for the Korean army generals went out of business, and the contract was awarded to Mr. Han Jong-chil, owner of a company called Hanguk Dokum located near Seoul in a city called Siheung.

Holding a third degree dan rank in Hapkido, a third degree dan rank in Taehan Kumdo, and a first dan in Hedong Kumdo, Han Jong-Chil is a maverick amongst Korean sword craftsmen. He said that while practicing Kumdo one day, he "felt ancient things about the sword. It drew me. It started as a hobby, and only later turned into a job."

Han Jong-Chil started his sword business back in 1986 having studied under the renowned Master Yeon In-moon, who in turn was trained by the legendary Jeong In-cho in Seoul. In addition, he went to Japan many times to see swords. In Japan, he saw that Japanese swords are made by a number of people, each making only a part of the sword, whereas in Korea, the work is more consolidated. The Japanese were impressed that in Korea one person could do so many different tasks at a high level of skill. One curious difference between Korean and Japanese sword-making methodology involves the difference between "folding" and "spreading" the metal. "While Japanese fold, the Korean way is to spread the metal," he said.

Like all masters of an art, he has gone beyond his teachers, making creative innovations in the crafting of his swords. For example, the hilt is bolted at the bottom (base), rather that held on with pins going through it. This is a unique design feature of Han Jong-chil's swords.

In past years, the curved swords he made for Korean generals (and admirals) were called *Samjeongdo*. According to a brochure on it:

The *Samjeongdo* saber represents the spirit of the Army, Navy and Air Force which has three goals to achieve: National Defense, Unification and Prosperity of the Fatherland." It is 100 cm in length. The hilt is 25 cm long and consists of basswood covered with sharkskin. The blade is 73 cm long, 3.2 cm wide, 7 cm thick and made of forged steel.

Starting next year a new sword will be presented to the generals, called *Sanjeong geom*. (Swords that end with the word *do* are single-edged weapons. Double-edged swords are called "*geom*") They would be handed over during the ceremony in January 1 and July 1, when officers are promoted to generals.

Han Jong-chil gets stainless steel for his swords from a variety of sources, including Korea, Japan, Germany, and Australia. Two companies he mentioned were Sam-mi and Hidachi.

Asked about his quenching procedure, he said that he uses oil specially produced for that task. He wouldn't be more specific. Masters all have their trade secrets!

Han Jong-chil also repairs swords of all kinds, even some very old ones, for customers.

Asked if Korean swordsmiths and manufacturers had an association of some kind, he responded in the negative. Asked why, he said that they were "very competitive."

His wife and daughter participated in the above interview. His daughter said "no" when asked whether she was going to continue in her father's footsteps and create a dynasty of sword-makers. A talented 19-year-old singer and dancer, she intends to be a performing artist. She is currently training with one of Korea's most popular female pop stars. In addition, her English is near fluent and she did most of the translating for this interview. Han Jong-chil's wife said that if were up to her, she'd have her husband just retire from the company now! He laughed at this and said he'd "thought about it." Han Jong-chil is 59, but looks about fifteen years younger.

Lee Seok-je's Sword Art Gallery

One of us visited Lee Seok-je's awesome sword museum/art gallery on June 10, 2006. Unfortunately, it was pouring rain and he wasn't there. However, his manager, Kim Ki-hwan, was present and talked about the owner :

Lee Seok-je has one of the finest private sword collections in Korea. He is one of the foremost authorities on sword history in Korea and has done a considerable amount of scholarly research about Korean sword history and crafting. He is also a consultant for the Military Museum in Seoul as well as the National Museum. His own large sword museum and shop, called: "Sword Art" in hip downtown Seoul, in a particularly upscale neighborhood called Insadong where he also owns a large traditional tea shop. The museum, shop and tea house are open seven days a week from 10 a.m. to 6 p.m. Lee Seok-je started collecting swords some twenty years ago and opened his business in February 2003.

He also appears to own a factory in Shanghai, China where most of his sword parts are made. Some assembly is done here in Korea. He has absolute control over design and quality of the swords he makes.

Lee Seok-je is a perfectionist with very high standards. He cannot and will not settle for something that is not perfect.

Above are stories about six of Korea's swordsmiths. Rumors vary as to the total number. Some say there are twelve; others have said there are as many as twenty. Several swordsmiths that we found declined an

interview. Our quest however is not finished. There are more Korean master swordsmiths out there.

Though there are great variations between Korea's few master swordsmiths and manufacturers, they also have many in common.

For one thing they are individuals of passion and character. These rare individuals have devoted themselves to furthering an art that was lost in Korea one hundred years ago. They have connected in some way with the primordial spirit of ancient Korea and brought it magnificently back to life through the crafting of their swords.

They are awesome scientists in their willingness to experiment with different procedures to make the finest swords. They are peerless technicians and artists in the awesome beauty of their work.

They are certainly rugged pioneers who have braved to seek their own paths in the jungles of the modern world. They have found that the beauty and power of the ancient world as expressed in swordsmithing and manufacturing is enough to sustain an existence in a world that is increasingly devoted to empty image-making and mindless materialism.

Let there be no doubt: these are great people who make great swords. Theirs are undervalued universe that deserves respect and admiration. No amount of money can really compensate for the love and passion that goes into their work. Swordsmithing is an industry, but more importantly, it's a science and a great art. It should also be a source of national pride and love.

Acknowledgements:

We would like to thank many people who helped us in researching and constructing this information. They include Ms. Lee Joung-hee (M.S. Jeonju University), who served as primary translator for almost all interviews. A Konyang University student, Kim Mi-young did most of the research finding the swordsmiths and manufacturers for us to interview. Many Konyang university students also helped translating, including Un Te-kun, Cho Jung-yun and Jang Kyung-hui. Finally, we need to thank the Korean swordsmiths and manufacturers who were—one and all—extremely kind, gracious, patient and generous.

Almost Korean

Soju, the Cultural Oxygen

The Little Neighbor with Wings

Please Don't Stop Eating

Three Wise People from the East

Korean Hospitality

Soju, the Cultural Oxygen

Craig White

I don't know what it is about *soju*, but it is the most mind-polluting form of alcohol on the planet.

Every time that I drink Korea's famous distilled liquor in abundance, I have blackouts and hellish mornings.

It always starts with doing the customary pouring. In Korea, it is customary to hold your ever-present soju shot glass with two hands, while the pourer pours and holds his wrist with his free hand. Then, someone shouts out "*Geonbae*!", which is similar to "cheers!", and everyone clinks their glasses and pounds back the poison, which is similar in taste to a tequila/vodka/gin hybrid. To be ultra-polite, if I was Korean and in front of someone elderly or my boss, I'd have to look away from the senior, when I down the shot; same thing with smoking. Often, younger Koreans will get up and leave the table to have a smoke, while the elders smoke and chat away at the table.

Anyway, as soon as your shot glass is empty, it is customary for someone else to fill it. In fact, I often notice Koreans' eyes scanning the table, during conversation, to make sure everyone is topped up. Another shot ensues. This time, someone says "One-shot!", which is Konglish for "down the hatch/chug-chug-chug". I down my shot and do the natural grimace and head-twitch. Someone refills my shot. On this night, I was sitting with a bunch of co-workers from the customer service department. There is a Korean-American rep in town and we're treating him to a night of drinking and eating.

The food is, of course, Korean. It never fails to amaze me how much mileage Koreans get out of eating ALL of an animal—intestines, feet, head, liver, live octopus, cow blood soup, even chickens' anuses. Yes, I've tried it. And it doesn't taste like chicken. For the most part, the stuff that's popular with foreigners is the galbi, bulgogi, samgyupsal, ie., the actual beef or pork that we are used to.

Tonight, however, we are sitting down to a simmering pot of potatoes, green onions, pig intestines, and pig's stomach lining.

Thank god that soju was going around. You know that you've been in Korea for too long when you can say to someone with a straight face, "The intestines taste ok, but what's the great marinade that they used on the chunks of stomach lining?"

We then went to a beer bar and drank pitchers of beer in front of a plate of *anju*. Anju is the customary food order that is expected when you go to lounge at a Korean bar. In this case, we ordered a plate of fruit. My memory begins to fade, as I was now mixing alcohol. *Soju*, with or without mixing, is always a night of mystery, after a certain point.

The Little Neighbor with Wings

Tonya Schwochert

One lovely spring break day, I sat down with a book in my local park. A pile of mussel shells lay at my feet from a bygone picnic, but I didn't care. It was a nice day.

Soon, a curious little girl began peeking at me through bushes, through trees...circling me, eventually ending up at the mussel shell pile at my feet. Little did I know that soon I would curse the day I met her.

She picked up my journal, laughed at the Roman letters, and flipped to a blank page. After five minutes of scribbling with my pen, she presented me a picture of the two of us. We both had large, glassy anime eyes, and we were wearing small dresses and angel wings. We were surrounded by hearts and puffy clouds. I had very impressive cleavage, and was being led by a small fuzzy dog on a leash.

I exclaimed over the picture, that it was actually quite charming. That is, before the little girl became my stalker and I burnt it in effigy.

"Teacher house!" she exclaimed. I pointed to the three-story apartment building over the Number One Mart and the Hi Oriental Brewery Bar. She pointed to herself, to me, then my house. "Teacher house!" she said. "Apple!"

I shook my head. I didn't have any apples. She insisted.

I had a sudden moment of worry when I realized that she was quite thin and perhaps needed that apple. Perhaps her mother didn't feed her and allowed her to roam the streets getting picked up by strangers. She did look quite scruffy, too, with stains on her striped shirt. I relented. I had just purchased some tangerines, anyway, that I could spare.

As we walked to my apartment, I wondered at the appropriateness of a student coming to my room. I decided that rules concerning students are quite lax in Korea, as evidenced by the swift smacks to the backs of their heads administered by my co-teacher.

Once in my apartment, I presented her a peeled tangerine. She ignored it and pounced on my computer. I decided she wasn't starving. She spent the next hour playing games online, most of which involved giving makeovers to little fuzzy dogs. After ornamenting dozens of pixilated dogs with sunglasses and curls, I told her that I had some illegal biological weapons-making to attend to and shooed her out.

But the next morning, promptly at 8 am, came a pounding on my door. "*Sonsangnim*!" a small voice shouted. "*Songangnim*!" I looked through the peephole. There she was, with her younger brother in tow.

I opened the door in my flannels. They pounced on my computer while I peeled more tangerines. This time, the boy, about five years old, drew me. I looked like a pumpkin with branches sticking out. The little boy babbled at me, smiling. The girl ran around my small apartment, at one point lifting the lid of my toilet, peering in, and exclaiming "wow!" They stayed a half-hour, the highlight being when the boy put on my Duff Beer hat and danced around the room to the Ramones, making noises like a Jawa. It was cultural exchange at its best.

I shooed them out, saying I had to go hunt stray cats in the alley with my Colt 45. Instead, I laid in bed all day, relaxing, with a couple of books to read. Relaxing, that is, until a couple hours later, when an assault upon my door made me freeze.

Pound-pound-pound. "*Sonsangnim*! *Sonsangnim*!" I didn't understand how her skinny arms had the strength. She jiggled at the doorknob, hoping to find it unlocked. "*Sonsangnim*!" she screamed.

I didn't move. I even held my breath. But she kept pounding as though she knew I was in there. Could she know? My fevered mind imagined her staking out a watch in front of my house, waiting to catch me if I ventured out. She found the doorbell and pawed it maniacally. After five minutes of throwing herself at my door, she left.

But that night, after I turned out my light to go to sleep, she was back. "*Sonsangnim*!" she yelled, pounding and ringing the bell. "*Sonsangnim*!"

"Go away," I whispered into the darkness. "Why do you love me so much? I didn't do anything for you. It's because of my computer, isn't it?"

She left, only to come again the next morning, and the next, and the next, with a couple afternoons thrown in for a good measure. Finally spring break ended, and I was glad to be back at school, away from the little girl.

On my first day back, I heard a knock on my classroom door. "*Sonsangnim*! *Sonsangnim*!" I couldn't believe it. She was a new student at my school. During the next few weeks she would slink around the hallways, occasionally popping her head into my office or my classroom. When I heard her voice screech "*sonsangnim*!" in the lunchroom, I shuddered and pretended not to notice.

The next time she pounded on my apartment door, I let her in and took out my calendar. I explained, in the bits of Korean I know that she should limit her visits to Sundays.

Distance made me start to warm to her. When the pounding on my door became less relentless, I began to look forward to her visits. As spring wore into summer, I would take my laptop outside and sit in the park, occasionally having visits by little Shi-Neui and Shi-Neung. One such day I was lying on a bench, typing, when Shi-Neui appeared. We ate *ddeokbokki* (Korean rice cakes seasoned with spicy sauce) and I played music on my laptop; when Buddy Holly came on, I taught her how to dance the Twist. I hoped that she'd get some use out of what I taught her, whether it be dancing to Buddy Holly or to speaking English. Collaborating, we have even come up with a new form of dance-slash-martial art, which I call "ballet-kwon-do." I was inspired when, one day after winning One Card, Shi-Neui did a graceful ballet maneuver followed by a tiger stance and knife block.

Coming back to Korea from a vacation in the States, I was overjoyed to find her in my hallway again. I had American coins in my pockets that I had saved for her.

I suppose that, like *soju* and *kimchi*, some things in Korea just take some getting used to.

Please Don't Stop Eating

Craig White

One thing I love about Korea and its people is the prevalence of food within their culture, for expressing gratitude, respect, or appreciation.

I had to laugh on the KTX. Once I was sitting next to an old lady and to her right was a Korean businessman younger than her.

I was dozing off and I woke up to her plopping an orange on my lap. I look up and see her Korean motherly look that comes off as "Don't even think about saying no to me. Eat it." I give my thanks and obediently eat her gift. She looks over to the Korean guy and does the same. No words. Just the plop of the orange on the lap. He does the proud Korean physical routine of 'no, no', and gives the orange back, and they do the unspoken back and forth with the orange, until she asserts her status by grabbing his hands and forcing him to take it.

Or what about the time I went to visit my girlfriend's mother at the hospital, at 10 pm. I brought a well-wishing gift and sat down with my friend next to her hospital bed. The next 10 minutes of Korean conversation centered around the mother's appreciation of me coming, and the expressions of food and eating, as a show of thanks. "Did you eat?", "When did you eat?", "What did you eat?","Here, let me peel this apple for you. Eat it. Eat it!" "Please continue to eat it.", "Ok, go to a restaurant and eat and come back.", "Please go.", "I don't care if it's 10 pm and you already ate dinner, please go eat something.", "Don't come back, unless you've eaten something." Reluctantly, we go out to eat and come back. "Did you eat?", "Was it enough?", "Are you sure?". We say our goodbyes and walk down the hall. The bedridden mother actually gets up out of her bed, comes to her door, and calls out to us, "Please make sure he eats something!"

At this point, I'm almost in stitches, as I'm trying not to take the situation too literally, but later my friend and I share a good laugh, as she explains that it is not uncommon to express respect through the incessant insistence of food and eating.

Three Wise People from the East

Maarten Meijer

English-speakers have long struggled to find a suitable translation for the mysterious emotional energy Koreans call *jeong*. In its many variegated forms—love, affection, passion, sentiment, sympathy, heart, attraction, bond—this is the emotion that pulsates through society. Me and my family have had samples from this deep spiritual reservoir through our encounters with three neighborhood Magi.

Park Kuk-ung–In a way, he is a "substitute" grandfather to my eldest son, Bobi. Although he really is not that old—I still remember his *hwoegap* (60th birthday) some time back—he has this timeless sophistication, old-style kindness, and gentlemanliness that you only find among people of a certain age and life-experience. He is even courteous in rush-hour traffic. Bobi used to visit him at the small hagwon he had, to brush up on his Korean. "Mr. Park"—as he is known among us—would always tutor him personally, even though he had several teachers there who could have done the job for him. He snapped pictures of my son in outrageous poses, celebrating a new taekwondo belt in his office. He is now retired but still swings by to pick up my son for lunch at the local galbi place.

Lee Yeon-ok –156 cm in height, she is barely taller than my 11-year-old son, Vasya. But whatever she lacks in physical stature, she makes up by the size of her heart. She has a beautiful smile, which she generously flashes on all those who enter Mugunghwa Hanewon, her husband's clinic of Oriental medicine named patriotically after Korea's national flower, but especially—or so I imagine—on me and the members of my family. She always has gifts to bestow: a box of pears, a jar of kimchi, a bag of dried squid, and Korean herbal soap. She is an accomplished artist and once gave us a scroll with one of her beautiful landscape paintings. We try to keep up with this avalanche of generosity: We invited her family to see 'Nanta' (drum performance) together. To everyone's delight, Vasya and my daughter, Renee, were invited on stage to drum along.

Park Hyeon-gi— For a long time, he was simply referred to as the "key-*ajeossi*" (*ajeossi*, meaning middle-aged man) in my family. He parks his diminutive van on the corner of our street and sells keys out of the back. He skips the rainy days but otherwise is always there. He is 84 years old, yet in crisp shape. His English is better than that of most Koreans. Apparently, he picked it up from American GIs during the War. Still, our conversations are mostly about the weather. When I pass by on my way to work, he cheerily shouts at me, "Nice day!" or "Too hot!" When my book "What's So Good about Korea, Maarten?" appeared, he held up a copy of the "Chosun Ilbo," which carried a positive review, and asked, "So how long are you going to stay in Korea?!" as if the nation would crumble were I to leave... And to Vasya he said, "You should become just like your father!"

Encore— And yes, then there is the *ajumma*. She generally comes in two types, A and B. The B-type pushes you off the escalator in the subway. But the A-type runs over with warmth and kindness. She holds your bag on her lap in a crowded bus; she gives free apples to your children on the street.

Korean Hospitality

Craig White

Almost Korean. That phrase gets uttered a lot, once you've been in this country for a bit and start to take on habits and the lifestyle of Koreans.

However, given Koreans' relatively limited exposure to foreign cultures, you can do something simple like using your chopsticks to pick up some noodles and the waitress will remark that "You're almost Korean!" She'll then go on to comment about how skilled you are with chopsticks. Or, you may say "hello" to someone in Korean and you'll hear someone nearby stammer to himself, "Jeez, he can speak Korean pretty well!"

Although it's done out of respect and politeness, being told that you are "almost Korean" for doing basic things, loses its appeal after awhile, until you start building a website on how to live, work and travel in Korea. Then you realize that you know more about some Korea-related things than the average Korean. For example, I just got an email from one of my Korean co-workers, asking where she can find a good *jjimjilbang* (Korean sauna) in the area. I found this to be surprising, as Koreans usually religiously search Naver or Yahoo Korea for their queries. Interesting.

On another note, while I was in Geochang to visit my friend and spend time with one of her students and his parents, I had a brush with the overwhelmingness of Korean hospitality. It sometimes steamrolls the unsuspecting foreigner.

The dad took us out for a pizza lunch. Now, you must understand something about Korean culture. There's the tradition of 'fighting' over who pays for the bill. Going dutch is not common. Rather, there is often a mock dispute/scuffle that happens when a restaurant/bar tab is to be paid. It is a respectful thing to pay for a bill. It is equally respectful to argue and shove (and sometimes even wrestle) with each other over who gets to pay the bill. Think of the stories of showing respect by haggling in India. If you don't haggle and you buy something outright, they are a little pissed, despite hosing you on the price. This mentality is shared in Korea, but only for duelling over who gets to pay the bill.

Being a foreigner, it is hard to figure out how much arguing, pushing, and rassling I need to do, if I am faced with someone who is very physically determined to pay. My Korean friend is always lecturing me that I need to really mix it up and get forceful (believe me, I'm not a cheap bastard, but I'm also not about to put someone in a full-nelson headlock, while swiping the bill away from him with my free toes.)

So after eating pizza, he gets up and quickly goes to the cashier to pay the bill. Cue from my friend to go over there and mix it up. Off I go. Shove-push-shove-argue-shove-argue. He wins.

Then we go off to play golf. I promised I would teach them the basics. Korea's golf courses are hellishly expensive, but tented driving ranges are everywhere, sometimes on top of buildings, due to lack of space. For $10, you can hit balls for a few hours. My friend was a natural and took to it right away. Lots of Koreans are quite good at driving a ball, considering that most of them don't get many chances to play on a real course. As we leave, the student's dad pays for all of us. Fight-push-argue, etc.

Later, we went back downtown to hang out at the family's cosmetics store, while we wait for the mom to finish work, so we can all go eat together. She starts spraying different colognes on the smell cards and asks me which ones I like. I can't really remember, as I thought she was just trying to occupy time until the store closed. The one I selected was Armani. Two minutes later, the bottle was gift-wrapped and given to me for free. Then again, there was the emphatic rejection/insistence on paying money, etc.

Next, we went out for galbi with the family to a local shop and drank and ate and drank and ate. They kept on ordering more food for me, even though I was clearly full. Koreans show respect and gratitude by making sure you are tremendously full. I think one could even puke in a pail next to the table, make yourself presentable, and then Koreans would often still encourage you to eat more, while topping off your soju shot glass.

Anyway, I kept a close eye on that bill. I had plans to excuse myself, go to the washroom and pay the bill while I was away from the table. But, later in the evening, the mother discreetly took the bill and put it underneath her purse, which was on the seat behind her. I knew we were down for a fight.

Sure enough, 30 minutes later, we were rassling. This time, it was a little more forceful, as we had a few drinks in us. I received a strong arm twist to let me know there was no way I was paying. Meanwhile, my friend is in the peanut gallery rooting me on to be more insistent that I pay.

To top it all off, it was time for me to go find a motel. Whenever I stay in Geochang, I usually prefer this small one in the downtown backstreets, because it is cheap and has the Internet in the room. The parents scoffed at that idea and said that they were taking me to a nicer place. My friend and I exchanged looks as we sensed another bill fight coming up. We pulled up in front of one of the nicer hotels in Geochang. The dad jumps out and scurries off to the lobby while I was dealing with the hot air coming out of my friend's mouth, again telling me to make sure that I pay. By the time I run into the hotel, I see funds being transacted to have me stay in the VIP room (only room remaining) and we tussled again for a few minutes. He dragged me all the way up to the room and made sure I was ok. I was fine except for the bruises from all that Korean hospitality.

Daily Encounters

The Wonders of Fusion Life at Jjimjilbang

Gosiwon Fever

The Weekend Traveler

The Eyeful Islands of the South, Oryukdo

Culinary Observations

Getting Fortunes Told

Korean Birds under Threat of Extinction

Feeling Chungnam

A Walk from a Temple to the City

Enchanted by the Sudden Cheongju Morning

The Wonders of Fusion Life at Jjimjilbang

Chad Walker

To me, *jjimjilbang*, or Korean-style saunas, offer one of the most unique and convenient ways to experience Korea. I like them so much I had my last birthday party there!

The word *jjimjilbang* can be broken down into the two words *jjimjil* (a Korean word meaning poultice, or compress) and *bang* (a Sino-Korean word meaning room, or chamber), hence its common translation as "sauna."

So why might a sauna be one of the most unique and convenient things in Korea? Well, let's start with what a *jjimjilbang* is not. It is not simply an adjunct to a health club, gym, or hotel. It is not simply a hot spring, such as those found all over Japan or Arkansas. And finally, it is not simply a massage parlor.

It is, to be sure, all of the above, plus more.

This photo shows us in one of the open areas having cake and drinks. The birthday cake is the only thing brought in from the outside. Notice the difference in color of clothes: brown for males and orange for females. All of the *jjimjilbang*s that I have visited will separate the *jjimjilbang* attire into two colors according to gender.

Another picture of guests relaxing and watching a World Cup game.

Sleeping is one of the most popular things to do at a *jjimjilbang*. The floors are warmed by ondol (a floor-heating system, the traditional way of heating rooms in Korea), eliminating the need for a blanket, and both traditional-style wooden and modern foam rubber pillows are available.

This picture is dark because it was taken after midnight, when it officially becomes "lights out." As there is no limit to the length of time you can stay per admission to a *jjimjilbang*, which usually costs around 6,000 to 8,000 won (6 to 8 dollars) per person, it is common for travelers and students to use them as cheap alternatives to hotels. Entire families often come to spend many hours as well, as the numerous amenities provide something that can be enjoyed by all age groups. This picture above shows a teenager lying on a blanket reading through a pile of comics.

Gosiwon Fever

Craig White

I have to get the hell out of this gosiwon. It's cheap and all, but it's driving me nuts. The paper-thin walls, cellphone alarm clocks of all different songs going off at different times are making me crazy. There is this new woman on my floor who has to get up at 6 a.m. for a shower every day and she makes a helluva racket, blowing her nose for 10 minutes, waking up all 30 people on the floor watching TV. Then when it's finally time for her shower, she has to go find the gosiwon manager to turn on the hot water boiler. He sleeps in one of the rooms, but she hasn't figured out which one yet. And his cellphone number is in big bold in the front office window. But she has to call out on our floor of over 30 rooms, every morning.

'*Sajangnim* (manager)! *SAJANGNIM*!! Bola kashipnee-bish-bam-boom-blah-blah juseyo (please turn on the hot water)!!'

Unfortunately, this culture is too polite and tolerant to stick their heads out of their doors and say 'Shut the HELL up!' And I'm too half-asleep to compute how to say it in Korean. So everyone just mumbles and gripes audibly to themselves.

Then the guy next to my room has to wake up and eat a bag of chips at 7 am. *Ruffle, ruffle, ruffle* *pause* *crunch, crunch, crunch, lip*-smack, lip-smack *pause* *ruffle, ruffle, ruffle* *pause* *crunch, crunch*, closed-mouth internal crunching noise, lip-smack, repeat ad infinitum.

Then I have to go to the washroom for the third time that morning. But it's two floors up and I have to get dressed first. Because it's an ordeal, I decide to just hold it in while trying to go back to sleep, which leaves me writhing and contorting on my super-size single bed. But the onset of pee-pee dance eventually begins and I have to scramble to get clothes on, to look presentable as a foreigner should, while sprinting up two flights of stairs past the bleary-eyed Koreans who may or may not have ever seen a white guy up close, let alone one who has a death grip on his groin.

The good thing is that I have free high speed internet access. But the fan from the laptop heats up the poorly-insulated room like a sauna. So I have to sit here naked, getting bitten by mosquitos that sneak in through the air conditioner vent. And these buggers are as clever as the Road Runner. I can't smack any against the walls or with both hands, as that will wake up everybody. So I feel compelled to do this one-handed air grab for 20 minutes.

I swear to god that the people who live in gosiwons must be on the poverty line, as I don't know where the discipline would come from to live here long-term. But, I'm out as soon as I have time to look around for a better place.

The Weekend Traveler

Peter Garnhum

Enjoying a packed lunch on top of the fortress wall running through Mt. Bukhansan National Park.

This is one of my favorite spots, just a few minutes below the main peak, Baekundae (836 m) - the view of Seoul to the east AND west on a (rare) clear day is unbeatable. Of course, it's not exactly a secret spot, either. Koreans come here in droves during the fall hiking season! I was always amazed and impressed that you can get to such a beautiful hiking area by public transportation.

After a particularly long and rowdy Saturday night in Sinchon, what better way to nurse a hangover than with that good old traditional farmers' rice wine, *dongdongju*? The *gamjajeon* (potato pancake) arrived right after this. We took a break from wandering the surprisingly engrossing Korean Folk Village (Minsokchon) near Suwon.

I caught this very telling juxtaposition of new and old Korea during a spring trip to Gyeongju. Similar images of contrast seem to be all over Korea.

Not technically a Korean shot, this one was taken on Kuta Beach on Bali. Anyone who's ever been to Kuta will tell you that the beach touts and vendors are perhaps the world's most persistent. After saying "No thanks" about 50 times, I caved and had this design done up by a temporary tattoo artist. I actually had to sketch it out for him. I think he was happy to keep the template so he could try selling it to Korean tourists.

Insadong, the traditional street, is always good for a Sunday afternoon, whether for shopping, eating, or simply spotting awe-inspiringly large novelty bottles of hooch. This was during the Makgeoli Festival, a great opportunity to sample the different varieties of the "unrefined rice wine." If only this bottle were real, it would be enough to ensure a year's worth of crippling hangovers.

The Eyeful Islands of the South, Oryukdo

William Jackson

All over Korea, there are lots of stray cats. Cats that have been abandoned by their owners and then they have managed to multiply in the wild. Oryukdo Island has its fair share of wild cats, although they seem to be a lot more larger, I guess due to scraps from the many fish restaurants, and also from the many bags of dumped food waste that seem to get dumped here. I liked the lazy look of the cat here gazing out into the distance. It kind of reflects the serene slow-paced aura of the island.

These two islands are part of the Oryukdo chain of islands. The name translates to five (*oh*) and six (*yuk*). This is because when the tide goes out there are 5 islands, but at high tide, 6 islands are visible because one of the islands resembles two by the eye. Many people visit this place for its breathtaking scenery, especially at sunset because of its history and sheer beauty. Also the area is famed for the quality of its seafood and numerous fishing opportunities.

I used a tripod and a 30-second exposure for this shot. On the horizon, there are several lights. These belong to squid boats, a sight that is very characteristic all along the Korean coast. The squid are attracted to the bright lights and are caught in thousands. Those outdoor lights on the island belongs to the Oryukdo Island lighthouse.

This part of Busan is the beach area of Oryukdo, Yongho-Dong, Busan. To me it is a place of curiosity and amazement. At the moment, a huge complex of apartment blocks are being built on the site, but previously, it was a whole district that had been laid to waste over the years. Many years ago, the place was a leper colony, but as the need for living space increased, the lepers went elsewhere. Many people flocked to this area and a thriving furniture business was created. But during the eighties, the businesses failed and people flocked to the more urban parts of Busan in pursuit of better jobs and living conditions partly because the area was a little isolated from the rest of the city. Over the years, many buildings became vacant, unused and derelict. The area became a ghost town with only a handful of residents deciding to stay.

In this photo, I was attracted to the contrast between the young man and his 'fashionable' clothes and the equally bright, but weathered colors of the ruined building. This man is not a resident, but one of the many visitors who frequent this part of town for the beautiful sights of Oryukdo.

During the 'ghost town' years, many people took the opportunity to fill many of the houses with an unbelievable amount of trash, and some decided to lay waste to the buildings and cause a good deal of vandalism. The home of this large collection of fire extinguishers is actually the local fire station which has long since been abandoned. Until recently, it was a small business dealing with recycling used fire extinguishers, but the owners eventually gave up on the project.

Culinary Observations

Don Oberdorfer

During the 4 years (1993-97) when I was writing my book, "The Two Koreas: A Contemporary History," I made 11 trips to Seoul for interviews and research. I nearly always stayed at the Seoul Hilton because it was attached by a tunnel to a Daewoo building that houses the Institute of Social Sciences. It was my unofficial host, that arranged my appointments and helping in many ways.

When I had no other lunch plans and felt I needed a reality fix, I would walk down the hilll to the nearby Southgate Market. There I would sit on a wooden stool outside one of its small restaurants in a small alley, eating Korean pancake, spicy beef stew with potatoes and vegetables, washed down by OB beer. Frequently other westerners would stop to inquire, "Is it safe to eat here?" My response was that I had been so used to it for many months, that I had suffered no ill effects. I simply appreciated the food and ambiance.

Getting Fortunes Told

G. Nikitas Brountas

From the look on his face, it seems as though this kid takes what the fortuneteller is saying quite seriously. I really wish I knew what was being said.

How big is fortunetelling in Korea?

According to an article by Chosun Ilbo, Some 450,000 fortunetellers and shamans ply their trade across the country, with the industry estimated to be worth 2 trillion won (US$2 billion)—roughly around the same level as the movie industry, which recorded 2.3 trillion won in 2004. The fortunetelling market is newly diverse. Once mainly the domain of housewives and public servants, the vagaries of the future now interest college students, office workers and professionals.

Getting your fortune told was free at the onset of spring (Ipchun Festival-the day when I took the photo above), so there was quite a line of people waiting to see what the future holds for them.

Korean Birds under Threat of Extinction

Tim Edelsten

The black-faced spoonbill was a good enough reason to justify extending my stay in Korea. A reed-fringed swamp among the bulldozers, not 30 minutes away from my *hagwon* (private institute), proved to be probably the best site in the world to see this elegant, splendid, prehistoric-looking and globally endangered bird, teetering on the brink of extinction. This truly is a Korean bird, dependent on the nation's relatively undamaged coastline.

When I first arrived in this fascinating country as another stop along my world tour, I had little idea that I would experience a diversity of landscapes in pursuit of special and rare wild birds. Gloriously vast mudflats teeming with shorebirds, alluring mountains hosting melodic songbirds, enchanting owls, the haunting cries of red-crowned cranes and skeins of noisy geese filling the winter air-this is the charm and pride of Korean nature.

I was charmed and surprised to hear people recall age-old songs featuring swallows, frogs and Watercocks. They seemed to belong to a time before Koreans were urbanized and lived in cities with every modern technology. As I dug deeper, I found the culture was rich in exciting myths of tigers and bears. It is known that the relationship between human beings and nature that bore Korea. I hope Korean will rediscover the significance of their nature.

I soon adopted Songdo, in Incheon, as my antidote to breakout from the anxiety I felt from Seoul. Glistening estuaries filled with life, stretched afar is a treasure in proportions unique to Korea. People gathered shellfish in thick mud, and not a sound broke the timeless peace of the rushing tides except for the piping flocks of shorebirds. Curlews and sandpipers gorged themselves on the rich supply of food. It was here that flocks of Black-faced Spoonbills, a charismatic but severely threatened bird with only a world population of around one thousand individuals, gathered every spring. This bird is truly a national speciality-Gangwha Island and Songdo are perhaps the best places on earth to see it. Songdo is also the home to the delicate and entrancing Saunders's Gull and the nesting colony was one of the last of this species known worldwide. As I fixed my telescope on the distant Oystercatchers and plovers, people were literally amazed to realize there were so many beautiful birds here. "I thought it was just mud" someone once told me. Sadly, this untouched land most valuable to wildlife, is also the cheapest and most readily available to be developed under.

As you may have guessed, the paradise was short lived. In the two years I have visited that site, bulldozers and barbed wire set about transforming it into the new, aspiring hub of Asia. Expanses of mudflat alternately washed and exposed by the tide, and harvested by fishermen, were concreted over in months. Apartment blocks suddenly reached skywards to the resounding slatter of jackhammers. This mirrored the situation a couple of hours drive to the south.

When I first visited Saemangeum (a project to develop 33km long tide embankment and land in Gunsan, Kimje, and Buan, Jeollabuk-do Province) I could scarcely believe that a pristine, unspoiled vista still survived in the 21st century. Great flocks of wading birds unrivalled anywhere else in Asia, including the globally endangered sandpiper, filled the view. There was something primeval about Saemangeum in autumn. You could find long lines of bar-tailed godwits, freshly arrived after non-stop 11,000km flights, finally dropping to refuel on shellfish. Waves of falcons preyed on them from the clear blue skies. It was truly an ecological jewel and a magical sight; a place where birds lived in rich variety, signaling a healthy environment fit for people as well. As the final debris filled in the 33km seawall in April of 2006, extinction looms for the sandpiper, and a way of life for birds and people dependent on the mudflats has passed away. This will also clearly impact the Korean fishing industry. Fish used these extensive mudflats to spawn, in a crucial stage of their life cycle.

Saemangeum now is a dustbowl strewn with vast banks of lifeless seashells and the debris of construction. Not far away at Gunsan, land reclaimed years ago lies empty, idle, and disused. Companies signed their contracts, made their short term profits, and moved on.

The western islands—Eocheongdo, Socheongdo, Seungbongdo, Muuido and Baengnyongdo are accessible by ferry from Incheon. Picturesque and quiet, many have populations of friendly but tough people, busily plucking a living from the sea. The men work hard on fishing boats by night; while the women gather seaweed and other nutritious delicacies from the shore by day. It is on these outposts that a startling variety of migrating songbirds crossing the sea stop to rest. Birds flying from nesting grounds as far north as the Arctic simply drop out of the clouds onto these islands, exhausted. This scene is a birdwatcher's dream. The beauty of these islands, topped with pines and fringed by red rocks and deep blue seas, is a delight to behold. I can only hope that the current mad rush to road-building and construction does not steal the essential character of these places.

January of 2004 was perhaps the most chilling I have felt in Korea, yet the most splendid. From Busan to Pohang and beyond, the Guryongpo peninsula was ravaged by savage winter gales that seemed to tear right through you. The pretty fishing villages, of colourful boats and sparkling bays were a visual feast, set against the gigantic rolling waves of the cobalt deep blue East Sea. What a different character that coast has compared to the murky shallows of the west!

The broad river-valleys of Gangwon-do, flanked by thick forests and tumbling streams on all sides, is without doubt the unspoilt playground—the wild west of the nation. In winter, these waterways are home to another of the world's more threatened wildfowl, the immaculately-ornamented, scaly-sided merganser. A rare duck with a world population of only four thousand, it graces these quiet rivers with its proud and fierce appearance every winter. Sadly, these very rivers are being cemented and banked, made into lifeless concrete troughs by what seems like an overzealous construction industry, committed to needless projects in the name of "flood prevention". This doesn't make sense. Rivers and streams edged with marshes and natural vegetation not only absorb much more floodwater than concrete trenches, they also sieve and purify the water. Maintaining natural vegetation provides a home for fish, frogs and insects, while removing it leaves barren waterways with far lower water quality. How much of the endless construction in the country is really necessary, or is it simply for the sake of providing jobs?

If you asked me to name the most beautiful place in Korea, I would insist on it remaining a secret. But let's just say it is somewhere along the untouched Imjin River that snakes along the DMZ. A fresh covering of snow glistening in the sharp winter sunlight lends a magical quality to the radiant golden reed beds and russet woodlands. The children skate on the ice here, and the occasional fisherman shows off his swollen catch of fish from the clean sparkling waters of the Imjin. In winter, lazy groups of massive black cinereous vultures, another threatened species, circle and soar overhead. Noisy flocks of geese fluster in every rice paddy. The aura the birds create is aplenty of life and beauty. The neighboring DMZ, undisturbed for decades, is thought by scientists to be a treasure trove of animals that have long vanished from South Korea. I hope it will always be the preserved home of the Siberian tiger, half-moon bear and Goral antelope. It is the 21st century, and we now have the last few remaining representatives of these wonderful creatures.

Korea must develop, but it need not be at the cost of destroying all of its last wild places and natural inheritance for short-term financial gain. With planning, it is entirely possible for Koreans to reserve a place for their birds and animals for future generations to enjoy. And nevertheless it is still possible to have nature reserves, clean air, pure water, tidal estuaries, and the birds that enrich our lives. These are real resources that we depend on in so many ways and I would urge people to develop an interest in nature.

Feeling Chungnam

Chris Van den Broeck

Downtown Cheonan on a Saturday Evening

The building on the right is the Arario Art Gallery, owned by a Damien Hurst nut. That piece by the window is by Hurst, which reportedly cost the owner more than 100 million won.

A Sunflower at Oeam Folk Village

Situated near Asan, Chungnam Province. Oeam Folk Village differs from a lot of the other folk village in Korea insofar as families actually live and farm there.

Bridge at Gungnamji Pond, Buyeo, Chungnam Province

Gwangduksa Temple Figurines

You can find little guys like these at almost every temple in Korea.

Icicles

They hang from the intricately painted eaves on a cold winter morning at Gakwonsa Temple, Cheonan, Chungnam.

A Costumed Performer at the General Lee Sun-shin Festival

The performer takes a bit of a rest at the General Lee Sun-shin Festival in Asan, Chungnam.

A woman praying at Gakwonsa Temple

Buddha's Birthday at Gakwonsa Temple

A little girl puts her artistic skills to work. She was one of many that day to color the pictures the monks had provided.

A Walk from a Temple to the City

Peter Carney

By the Temple

Women at a local temple relax and take a minute to escape from the hustle of the city. They take the weight of their feet and watch the world go by.

Roof Tiles Temples

A new and larger temple was being built next to its older neighbor at Cheonwongsa Temple. The names of people are often written, painted or etched into roof tiles.

Jongno Alleyway

Seoul is a modern metropolis of a city but if you observe discreetly, there are many little alleyways of life sandwiched between apartment blocks and shopping streets. This little alley in the Jongno 3(sam)-ga area is just one of many.

Myeongdong

Fashion-conscious teenagers clothed in designer brands flock to Myeongdong. Myeongdong is one of the main shopping districts in Seoul full of designer brands and labels. Life as a Korean teenager can be tough, and many teenagers use retail therapy as a release from the stress of academic work. Whatever the form of relaxation, you can guarantee that there is always a cellphone involved!

Noryangjin

The biggest fish market in Seoul that never sleeps, providing restaurants and residents with a range of seafood.

Enchanted by the Sudden Cheongju Morning

Rachel Harris

Mt.Songnisan, Cheongju by Night

On a very early morning in Cheongju, I made a sudden decision to go to Mt. Songnisan. I got a 6 a.m. bus with a gaggle of halmonis (elderly women) It was bone-cold and I shivered so much that I had to press my elbows against two trees to get this. It was the last day of fall splendor in a Korean park.

Contributors

David Smeaton Australian photographer and English teacher, Bundang
http://www.super-dave.com

Michael Hurt American photographer and media artist, Seoul
http://metropolitician.blogs.com

Ralph Pruszynski Canadian English Teacher, Seoul
http://www.pbase.com/koreanczyk

Mary Crowe American writer for Korea Times
http://www.maryeats.com

Joe McPherson American, freelance food writer, Seoul
http://www.zenkimchi.com

Derek Winchester Canadian, photographer, Suwon

Aly Young former English Teacher, Anyang
http://alyinkorea.blogspot.com

Ben Voborsky photographer, Seoul
http://www.benvoborsky.com

Andrew White American lecturer, Induk Institute of Technology, Seoul

Nayan Sthankiya Canadian, photojournalist
http://www.nayansthankiya.com

Donald Anderson Canadian
http://www.efeele.com/vlog

Gregory C. Brundage Kim Dammers lecturers at Gonyang University, Nonsan

Craig White entrepreneur Daegu
http://www.galbijim.com

Tonya Schwochert English teacher, Suwon

Maarten Meijer the author of 'What's so Good about Korea, Maarten?'
Chad Walker American, student at Yonsei University

Peter Garnhum former teacher, Incheon

William Jackson English
http://www.flickr.com/photos/95582337@N00

Don Oberdorfer Journalist and author of 'The Two Koreas:
A Contemporary History' and Professor of Johns Hopskins University

G. Nikitas Brountas American, English teacher, Jeju-do

Tim Edelsten English

Chris Van den Broeck Canadian, Lecturer, Baesok College of Cultural Studies, Cheonan

Peter Carney photographer, Seoul
http://www.flickr.com/photos/94233847@N00

Rachel Harris English/Canadian, teacher, Daegu